D0307492

STOP ARGUING,
START TALKING

You may also be interested in the following Vermilion titles:

The relate Guide to Better Relationships by Sarah Litvinoff

The relate Guide to Staying Together by Susan Quilliam

The relate Guide to Sex in Loving Relationships by Sarah Litvinoff

The relate Guide to Starting Again by Sarah Litvinoff

The relate Guide to Second Families by Suzie Hayman

To obtain a copy, simply telephone TBS Direct on 01206 255800

STOP ARGUING, START TALKING

The 10 point plan for couples in conflict

Susan Quilliam
with relate

VERMILION
London

1 3 5 7 9 10 8 6 4 2

Copyright © Transformation Management Ltd and Relate 1998

Susan Quilliam has asserted her right to be identified as the author of this work.

All rights reserved. No part of this publication may be reproduced, stored in a retrieval system, or transmitted in any form or by any means, electronic, mechanical, photocopying, recording or otherwise, without prior permission from the copyright owners.

First published in the United Kingdom in 1998 by Vermilion
an imprint of Ebury Press
Random House, 20 Vauxhall Bridge Road, London SW1V 2SA

Random House Australia Pty Limited
20 Alfred Street, Milsons Point, Sydney,
New South Wales 2061, Australia

Random House New Zealand Limited
18 Poland Road, Glenfield,
Auckland 10, New Zealand

Random House South Africa (Pty) Limited
Endulini, 5A Jubilee Road,
Parktown 2193, South Africa

Random House UK Limited Reg. No. 954009

A CIP catalogue record for this book is available from the British Library

ISBN 0 09 181623 8

Printed and bound in Great Britain by Cox & Wyman Ltd, Reading, Berkshire

Papers used by Vermilion are natural, recyclable products made from wood
grown in sustainable forests.

CONTENTS

Acknowledgements

I wish to express my warmest thanks to everybody who has made this book possible.

To Julia Cole and Suzy Powling of Relate, who originated the idea for this book, and whose energy got the project off the ground.

To Sarah Bowler, Derek Hill and Marj Thoburn of Relate who sponsored and supported the project as a celebration of Relate's sixtieth anniversary.

To Sarah Sutton, Joanna Sheehan, Margot Richardson, Nikki Cowan of Vermilion for speedily and professionally bringing the book to the printed page.

To Barbara Levy, my agent, for her continuing support, and to Lisa Eveleigh.

To Trevor Day for specialist scientific advice, Shaun McCarthy for specialist dialogue advice and John Hollis for specialist computer advice.

To all the Relate counsellors who gave me their time, energy, inspiration and experience, particularly John Brazier, Ronnie Briggs, Karen Bullough, Kevin Chandler, Jo Goodwin, Val Gough, Maggie Greaves, Jenny Green, Elizabeth Hargreaves, Rosie Hitchins, Denise Knowles, Jill Lockhart, Carole Pearson, Carol Pocknell, Suzy Reindorp, Lucy Selleck, Sue Shaw, Joanna Vials, Janet Ward.

A special thank you to all the couples who had the courage to share with me their experience of conflict, resolved and unresolved.

To June Bulley for her administrative excellence and her ability to fend off distractions.

To Corinne Sweet, Sarah Litvinoff, Suzie Hayman, Harriet Griffey and all the members of the Relationship Authors' Group for their ongoing support.

And a final thank you to my husband Ian, who as always makes all things possible.

HOW TO USE THIS BOOK

This book is a practical guide to stopping painful arguments in your relationship. Its ten steps combine the wisdom of actual couples and Relate counsellors in a way that you can use to help yourself. Particularly, the book will support you to understand what happens when you're in conflict, and learn practical skills to manage that conflict.

You'll get most out of the book if you:

- work through the steps in sequence.
- think about the explanations, the couple's stories and the worked examples of conversations.
- allow lots of time while you are completing each step, and between each step, to take in what you've understood.
- regularly practise the skills that you learn.
- do the tasks that are included in each step.

As you complete the tasks, turn to Step 10 and answer the questions listed there for each step. This will help you to keep track of what you have learned and your progress in resolving conflict. (You will need to record the relevant information in a separate note book.)

You'll also get most out of the book if both partners in your relationship work through it together, doing the tasks, then comparing notes. But if this isn't possible, you can still benefit. If even one of you starts to understand what is happening and gain skills, your partnership will improve. If you're working through the book on your own, skip the tasks that are marked 'work together'.

Bear in mind that it is often very hard, if not impossible, to try changing your relationship in the middle of a major crisis. Such emergencies may include a death in the family, taking exams, or even just moving house. If you are actively at each other's throats, try calling a peace treaty until the crisis is over. Then, when life is less stressful, make efforts to improve your relationship.

A final point. This book has been written for you to use without the aid of a counsellor. But it doesn't replace the expert help that counselling provides. If your partnership shows signs of needing such help – if there is violence, drug or alcohol abuse; an ongoing affair; constant bad feeling; an inability to talk to each other at all – do contact Relate (see page 189) for the support you need.

DECIDE TO CHANGE WHAT YOU'RE DOING

So you have arguments. The first thing to realise is that you're not the only one.

The fact that you and your partner differ and disagree, and that your disagreements lead to conflict, may be painful, but it's normal. And the fact that your relationship is painful doesn't mean that you're the only couple in the history of the universe to feel like this. It doesn't mean that you're inevitably failing. What it does mean is that you and your partner are two of many millions of people in the world today who have never been shown how to handle conflict.

Of course, your situation will be special to you alone. It could be that you snipe about anything and everything; you pass the marmalade and it causes trouble. It could be there are only a few tricky issues – money, kids, friends, sex – but when these come up, it's as if World War Three has broken out. It could be that when you and your partner disagree it's never about anything significant, and afterwards you suffer complete amnesia about what on earth made you scream at each other. Or it could be that your memories are all too active, and that every argument leads inexorably back to the same issue, such as the same unresolved betrayal of decades ago.

You'll have individual patterns to your conflict. Arguments may erupt quickly but then die away. Fights may build slowly, lead to a weekend's solid arguing, and then leave you traumatised for weeks. There may be hardly-noticeable, daily skirmishes; or brick-wall, month-long sulks. Your conflict may have started a few months ago, a few years ago, or may have been hovering since the day you met, a lasting and exhausting burden.

But whatever the patterns, one thing will be permanent: the pain. Perhaps it's only a minor irritation, but it spoils an otherwise happy relationship. Perhaps it's panic: that these arguments mean you have to split up. Perhaps it's occasional bubbling fury, so that you're scared you'll do something you'll regret. Or perhaps it's total exhaustion and disillusionment, a feeling that you've been to hell and back.

Now you want the pain to stop. You've reached a point in your conflict where you think 'enough is enough'. That's good. It means something's going to change.

Typically, partners reach their 'enough' point for two reasons. Either something from within your relationship has triggered you into realising that you want and deserve better than you already have. Perhaps you've had one argument too many, have gone over some sort of threshold, and have realised that it's all too much. Perhaps you or your partner has been ill, and all at once you've realised, along with the thought of death, that you don't want to live like this any more.

Or, something has happened to make you look around. Perhaps for the first time you're viewing the relationship from the outside and realise that what you thought was a stumbling but basically happy relationship is much worse than that. Perhaps a friend has jokingly commented that 'you two should give lessons in arguing'. Perhaps you've concluded that your arguments are much worse and much more destructive than any other couple's, and are going to split you up. Perhaps you've met a couple who seem always to delight in each other's company, and you've started to panic that it will never be like that for you.

Whatever your reasons, you have finally called 'stop'. And though it may feel like the end of the road, in fact it's a good beginning. The very fact you're reading this book means that things are changing. You've felt vulnerable, but now you're taking charge. You've been through a hard time, but now you're doing something about the problem.

WHAT'S POSSIBLE, WHAT'S NOT

The first thing to do is to look at what's possible. Conflict can feel incredibly out of control. There's so much emotion around, the arguments seem to spring from nowhere at the drop of a plate, and whatever you try seems to trigger off another fight. Because of all this, it's tempting to want a magic solution. It's tempting to want the wave of a wand that will miraculously and instantly remove all differences, all disagreements, all debates, all arguments, all painful feelings – and then replace these things by a perfect and endlessly happy union.

The bad news is that such a magic solution is impossible. The good news is that it's also undesirable. If you had a relationship without difference, without disagreement, without debate and without any painful feeling, then what you would have would be hell, not heaven. You would have a relationship with no strength, no heart, no potential for growth, and certainly no humanity. Here's why.

You can't have a relationship without . . .	You wouldn't want a relationship without . . .
. . . **difference**: all human beings are intrinsically different, in background, upbringing, personality, feelings, needs and wants.	. . . **any differences**: it's complementarity not similarity that makes relationships work. Successful couples balance out each other's weaknesses and vulnerabilities.
. . . **disagreement**: disagreement is a natural result of difference; as everyone sees the world slightly differently, people will always disagree on some level.	. . . **any disagreement**: that's only possible if one partner always pushes down needs and holds back on opinions. Remember the Stepford Wives?
. . . **debate**: if disagreement is inevitable, then debate about those disagreements are inevitable too. The only question is whether that debate is constructive or destructive.	. . . **any debate**: done properly, talking issues through is the best way to create solutions that meet both your needs.
. . . **painful feeling**: emotions aren't actually controllable. They pop up whether you want them to or not. It's only the awareness and expression of those emotions that you can control.	. . . **any painful feeling**: painful feelings are a vital sign something needs sorting out. If you don't feel the feelings at all, you don't have advance warning of the problems. Then you can't sort them out.

If all the things mentioned above aren't possible or desirable, what is? What can you do to solve the problem of argument?

What you can do is to change so that you see the differences between you and your partner as positive, not irritating – realising that couples who are different have more to offer each other and the world.

You can learn to disagree in a way that doesn't hurt by valuing each other's opinions and taking them into account. You can develop ways of debating that don't involve fighting by avoiding destructive debating methods such as nagging, sniping or sulking. You can learn to value your feelings as a good early warning system, and make them work for you.

You can learn to believe that you've a right to have your needs met, and then have them met. You can learn to talk through the issues and resolve them to mutual satisfaction.

And because you're doing all this, you can reach a point in your relationship where you feel bad very rarely because there's little in your relationship that needs sorting out. What you can do is to develop a way of managing conflict constructively and positively rather than destructively and negatively.

THE OPTIONS ARE . . .

Let's be more specific – as this section of the book is about being specific. It's about starting to understand just what's wrong with your relationship and how it can be put right. Particularly, it's about seeing clearly what your options are in putting it right. It's about realising exactly what the result will be if you work through all the ten steps; and it's about deciding whether working through the steps is something you want to do.

Joanne and Dan have been together for eight years. They're at the stage where, quite simply, they're starting to irritate each other a good deal of the time.

The kids are in bed, Dan's been tidying up in the kitchen, Joanne has her feet up on the sofa with the television on and the evening paper in her lap. Dan walks in, reaches for the remote control and switches channels.

What they think . . .	What they say . . .
Joanne thinks 'He always does that.'	Joanne says in an irritated tone 'Hold on, Dan, I was watching that!'
Dan thinks 'I can never do anything right with her nowadays.'	Dan says in an irritated tone 'But you're reading the paper.'
Joanne thinks 'He's doing this deliberately.'	Joanne says in a patient voice but with eyes cast up to heaven 'Reading the paper? No, the paper was on my knee. I was actually watching the television. Is that a problem?'
Dan thinks 'She's treating me as if I was stupid.'	Dan says wearily 'All right, all right. Give me a break, Jo. I've had a hard day.'
Joanne thinks 'Why does he always blame me?'	Joanne says sharply 'Hard day? You're not the only one. So is it OK if I watch my gardening programme, then?'
Dan thinks 'There's no point in even trying here.'	Dan says angrily 'Do I have any say in the matter?'
Joanne thinks 'I'm certainly not going to let him watch what he wants, whatever it is.'	Joanne says sharply 'All right, then, tell me what you want to watch.'
Dan thinks 'If I hurt, I'm going to make her hurt too.'	Dan says sulkily 'There's no point . . . you never listen.'
Joanne thinks 'How on earth did all this happen?'	Joanne says wearily 'I never listen? Why should I bother? All we ever do is fight!'
Dan thinks 'Here we go again.'	Dan says wearily 'Oh for heaven's sake, Jo, don't start . . .'

Now let's see how things could have gone if Joanne and Dan had been able to handle the conflict in a more positive way.

What they think . . .	What they say . . .
Joanne thinks 'He always does that.'	Joanne says in an irritated tone 'Hold on, Dan, I was watching that!'
Dan thinks 'I can never do anything right with her nowadays.'	Dan says in an irritated tone 'But you're reading the paper.'
Joanne thinks 'This could lead to an argument if we're not careful.'	Joanne says, with an effort to calm her voice 'No, love, I'm not reading any more. I was really looking forward to my gardening programme, and when you changed channels, I just snapped. I'm sorry'.
Dan thinks 'I understand she felt upset.'	Dan says more calmly 'I didn't mean to . . . I didn't realise . . . .'
Joanne thinks 'OK, he didn't mean to hurt me.'	Joanne says, feeling fine now 'No, I know you didn't. What did you want to watch?'
Dan thinks 'Let's see if we can work this out.'	Dan says, trying to respond to her 'How long does your programme last? I wanted to catch the film on the other side. I've had a rotten day; I need something mindless!'
Joanne thinks 'That's nice. Even though he's had a rotten day, he still tidied the kitchen.'	Joanne says comfortingly 'Mine's on from seven until half past. I'm sorry you're tired. Do you want to curl up here?'
Dan thinks 'She does care for me.'	Dan says in a relaxed way 'OK, shall we video your programme, or mine? I'm happy either way.'
Joanne thinks 'He's giving me a genuine option here, so what's the way to please us both?'	Joanne says positively 'Record the gardening. I'll watch it tomorrow when you're out.'
Dan thinks 'Great.'	Dan says lovingly 'Great. Why don't I set up the video? Then we can cuddle up and watch the film.'

The starting point for both those conversations was the same. But the conclusions were very different. Joanne and Dan handled things very differently in the second conversation from the way they did in the first – and they got much better results!

Rather than staying irritated, Joanne realised what was happening and made an effort to calm down and explain how she felt. Rather than going on the defensive, Dan listened to Joanne's explanation and tried to understand. Rather than lashing out or simply giving in, both found out what the other needed, then did their best to respond to those needs. They offered comfort, support – and managed to find a practical solution to the programme clash. Because of that, in the end, both got what they wanted and felt good about themselves and each other.

The fact is that all couples have differences, disagreements and conflict. It's the way you resolve this conflict that counts. Couples who always try to resolve disagreements with battles are the ones who leave each other traumatised, licking their emotional wounds or in the divorce court. Couples who never admit the differences are often the ones who, after twenty five years of marriage, suddenly turn a chainsaw on each other because there's so much unresolved fury.

But couples who manage their conflict constructively turn their differences and disagreements into allies rather than enemies. By finding solutions that work for both partners, and neither giving in nor giving up, couples like this not only help each other to be happy. They also develop a more effective relationship, combining their approaches and opinions, blending their individual strengths and neutralising their individual weaknesses.

So the way you handle conflict is a vital sign in assessing the health of your relationship. In fact, over the years, studies have shown that if you're married, the way you handle conflict is the most important predictor of whether you will divorce. It's more important and more reliable than whether the two of you are compatible in bed, whether you have interests in common – or even whether you feel you're in love.

> **Studies have shown that the way married couples handle conflict is the most important predictor of whether they will divorce.**

Negative conflict management: not recommended	Positive conflict management: the way to go
You both have needs and wants. Your needs and wants are different. You both feel uncomfortable about your differences. You both try to be heard and understood.	
But in negative conflict management . . .	*In positive conflict management . . .*
You allow yourselves to be overwhelmed by hurtful emotions; you may experience anxiety, anger, confusion.	You make your feelings work positively for you.
You're unaware of what's going on, and so simply defend or attack in order to survive.	You realise what's going on, and are able to turn the conflict in a positive direction.
You feel critical of each other, and don't even try to stop thinking critically.	You make a conscious effort to think positively about each other.
You express what you feel in a way that hurts, or you refuse to say what you feel, so creating even more bad feeling.	You express what you feel in a way that doesn't hurt each other.
There's no real listening going on, so you both feel unappreciated and resentful.	You show appreciation of each other's emotions and point of view, so each of you starts to feel understood.
Neither of you are truly aware of what you need, or believe that you don't deserve to have it, so don't express it clearly.	You're each aware of what you need, believe you deserve to have it, and explain it clearly – so giving each other a chance to help.
Each of you has his or her own agenda at heart – either to have what you want, to have 'the last word' in the argument, or to avoid trouble at all costs.	You negotiate to reach a win-win solution, one that meets both your agendas.

In the end, neither of you has what you wanted, or one of you has it all and the other feels resentful. Nothing's sorted out.	In the end, both of you feel that you gained most, if not all, of what you needed. The original issue is sorted out.
Afterwards, you feel worse about everything. Nothing's improved. What's happened has simply added to the problem.	Afterwards, you've both gained insights about yourselves and each other. You feel good. The relationship feels stronger. You're more hopeful about your future.
You fight again, with increasing frequency.	You resolve issues again and again, with increasing frequency.

So how do you learn to handle conflict well? In fact, you're already learning. By exploring what conflict is, and beginning to understand what it involves, you've already started changing things. The rest of this book takes you through the complete process: finding out why you argue, analysing how you argue, making your emotions work for you; learning to understand your partner; controlling an argument; learning to communicate and negotiate so that you both have more of what you want.

DO YOU WANT TO CHANGE?

'I was very jealous in those days. And somehow being engaged made it worse. Instead of feeling more secure that Stephanie was going to stay with me, I felt I had to fight off any other man who came near. She herself admits that she wound me up just to prove I loved her enough to do it. So we'd go down the pub, she'd start chatting, and we'd fight all the way home about whether she was being chatted up. One night we had words, she told me to stop the car, and she got out and started walking along the country road. I revved up and drove all the way home. Four hours later I was tearing my hair out, thinking she'd been murdered. In fact, she'd twisted her ankle in a ditch and landed in the Cottage Hospital. When I went to pick her up, we sat in the car for hours talking about whether we did want to get married. We worked out that if we did, we had to sort it, quickly.'

James

It's time to look at your own relationship and decide just where you stand on all this. How much of a problem is what you're already doing? And are you ready to start changing that?

! ════════════ *Task 1.1* ════════════

Where are you now . . . where do you want to be?

Read these questions and think about them on your own. Take it slowly. Take a few days perhaps, to review what's happening between you both, and to assess the scale of the problem. Make notes if you need to. Swap notes with your partner if you're able to.

Do you both see the problem in the same way?

How long have your arguments been going on? For example: recently, since a particular date, since the start of your relationship? Does the number of your arguments shift over time?

What do you see and hear happening when you argue? For example: sharp comments, shouting, sulking, silence, giving in to keep the peace? Think about what you do, and about what your partner does.

What pattern, in general, do your arguments follow? For example: big blow-up, slow build-up, constant nagging? If there's more than one pattern, then write them all down.

How do you feel when you argue? For example: frightened, angry, frustrated, sad, guilty, hopeless? How do you feel about your arguments? Have your feelings altered at all since your arguments first began?

Why do you want to change what's happening? For example, you may want to change because you're starting to get ill, becoming depressed, feeling bad about your partner, feeling bad about yourself, scared you'll split up. **(Forward to Step 10**, page 180**)**

What are your goals? What change would you like to make to the way you manage conflict? If things changed in the way you want them to, what would be different about the way you behave? How will life be when this change has happened? **(Forward to Step 10**, page 180**)**

!

Doing this task will have focused your thoughts. If you've swapped notes with your partner, this will have made things even clearer. And probably, you'll find yourself in one of three situations . . .

1 Perhaps one or both of you has realised that actually, you don't want to change the way you handle conflict. What you truly want is to be out of this relationship as soon as possible. This may seem like a sudden revelation. How could such a conclusion be triggered so quickly? But it could be that your reason for exploring your arguments was that you wanted a catalyst, to allow you to realise the truth, to allow you to make the break. If so, consider carefully. Talk to each other. Take advice. Perhaps read one of the other Relate guides that deal with your particular situation (see page 186). Perhaps go for counselling. If in the end your future lies outside your current relationship, then good luck on your new journey.

2 Perhaps one or both of you has realised that although your situation is painful, you don't have the energy or the motivation to change. You don't want to part, but changing the way you argue seems just too hard, too frightening. In fact, this is a worrying realisation. You are in conflict. And one of you at least is unhappy about those arguments. So if nothing changes, at least one of you and probably both of you will continue to be unhappy. Things will become worse, not better. Even if you've made up your minds that this time things will be different, that this time you'll never again be hurtful to each other, in fact you're being over-optimistic. Will-power alone doesn't stop arguments. However scary it seems, only learning new ways of thinking, feeling and behaving will do that.

3 Perhaps one or both of you wants to change what's happening. You want to start resolving your conflicts in a way that doesn't hurt. This is the most optimistic possibility. It means that almost certainly things will get better. But even so, you may be wary. What if trying to solve your argument problem means that you end up giving in to your partner all the time? What if you find you never have anything you want? What if you

find out you're incompatible? These are natural fears, but they're almost always unfounded. Learning to resolve your conflicts constructively rather than destructively typically means both of you having more of what you want; otherwise the system doesn't work. Learning to meet each other's needs usually means you feel more in tune with each other rather than less.

! ================ *Task 1.2* ================

Countdown to change

If you, alone or with your partner, have decided that you want to start to change the way you manage conflict, then you can make a start right away.

Think carefully about the ways you want things to be different and set a date by which you'll have made at least three improvements.

(Forward to Step 10, page 180) !

HELPFUL HINTS FOR CHANGING
COUPLES

'About three years in, the sex started to slide. He'd had a really bad time at work, couldn't get it up for a while, then I got frustrated and started to nag. Of course, he felt pressured, that led to rows, and things got worse. After about four or five months, realising how bad things were, my mum took the kids off our hands for a weekend and we went away. For the first time in months, we talked about us and how we felt. By the end of the week, we realised we were going to stay together, and that meant that we wanted to have sex again. It's taken a while and we've had to work pretty hard. He needed to learn that I wasn't going to blame him if he wasn't up for it, and I needed to learn not to pressure him just because I was frustrated. But it's coming back slowly. The more we talk, the less we fight. The less we fight, the more we have sex.   Catherine

As you feel yourself making the decision to change the way you're handling your conflicts, take a moment to think about how that change might happen – and how you're going to handle it.

The first secret of success is to regularly create a clear picture of what you want. You know now what isn't possible, and you have a realistic appraisal of what is. You've begun thinking about your goals, so keep those goals in mind. See a clear representation of how you and your partner will handle your differences, how you'll resolve your disagreements, how you'll manage your conflict. Regularly take time to imagine yourselves calmly and happily meeting each other's needs; whether those needs are for a better way to make the supper, or a better way to make love.

Take things very slowly. By all means read this book from cover to cover now. But don't expect to shift your fighting habits over a weekend. It works best if you take your time. Re-read each section until you fully understand it. Do the tasks carefully, and think about what you learn from each. Practise the skills over weeks and months, not hours or days.

Equally, make changes one by one. Even a small change can make a big difference in time. So don't try to master everything at once. It works better if you tackle one skill, master it, then move on to the next one. Remember that if the next argument you have is even 2 per cent better than the one you last had, then it will only take fifty arguments before you've cracked it. And that number may well be just a tiny proportion of the arguments you've already had to suffer.

It's best not to even try changing in the middle of a major crisis. It's hard to cope with a relationship shift and an emergency at the same time. So if you're currently under a great deal of stress or supporting someone who is, then consider putting change on the back burner for a week or two until the pressure is off.

The final secret of success is to stick with it even if things are tough. It may be that at the start, while you're adjusting to new ways of behaving, you have more arguments rather than less. Or it may seem that you solve your problem completely and then find it comes back with a vengeance after a week or two. Don't panic. You're attempting to change ways you think, feel and behave that you may have been using for decades. You're trying to learn complex relationship skills that you may never have used before. It will take time and effort. It will be worth it.

WHERE ARE YOU NOW?

Step 1 has helped you start to explore what conflict is all about, to explore just what your conflict patterns are and to decide what to do next.

As you complete the tasks in this step, remember to turn to Step 10 and fill in the relevant sections there.

Move on to Step 2 when:

- you feel that you're starting to understand what relationship conflict really is.

- you've defined just where you are and where you want to be, by answering the questions on page 19.

- you've made up your mind that you want to change those patterns, to 'stop arguing and start talking'.

FIND OUT WHY YOU'RE ARGUING

'We were fine for thirty-four years. Then, just as the kids were off our hands and we were winding down, the arguments started. It was all about the canal boat; at first about how much to spend, then about what type of boat, then about where to moor it. Then we were into another round of arguments because he never seemed to want to work on it. I was at my wits' end.

'One day we were sitting on top of the boat, trying to fight quietly so the other people on the marina wouldn't hear, and he said "I don't want to be doing this. I don't want to give up on real life." We spent the whole night talking, about him being scared of retirement, and old age, and death. We worked hard on it. We came through. Thank God we realised what it was about before I gave up on him.'   Betty

An argument is a bit like a Russian doll, a Chinese puzzle or an onion. It has lots of layers, each tightly wrapped around each other. You may seem to be fighting about one thing. But the real issue may be several layers down. What you think you're arguing about is often not what you're really arguing about at all.

If you want to stop the arguments, you have to tackle them at the correct layer of the puzzle. There's no point in solving only the surface problem, only to discover that the deeper levels of problem are still there making trouble. In fact, once you do find out what is

---

What you think you're arguing about is often not what you're really arguing about at all.

happening underneath, it's sometimes not only obvious what you need to do. Sometimes, simply knowing what the root cause of the problem is means that you can change. Sometimes, knowledge is the key to rethinking your ways of managing conflict; as well as being able to stop in your tracks as a battle starts and think 'We don't need to be doing this, do we?'

THE ISSUE

On the outer layer of the puzzle is the most visible issue. This is the most obvious thing that springs to mind when you think about the reasons the two of you are arguing. It's usually practical, objective and very specific; a nitty gritty problem that you simply can't agree on.

These are the things that couples say they're most likely to argue about:

- Money: issues such as who pays for what? Who decides what we spend? Why don't we have more money? Why do we spend so much?
- Sex: issues such as how come you don't want it any more? How come you want it so much? What do we do when you want to do something in bed that I don't want? What sort of contraception should we use?
- Children: issues such as how many should we have, and when? If they're stepchildren, how do we handle things? Who pays for the child care? Who disciplines the children, and how?
- Family: issues such as whose relatives shall we visit, especially at Christmas? What should we do when grandparents interfere? Who has to do the caring when a parent is ill or old?
- Work: issues such as why do you spend so much time at work? Why do you never talk about your job? How come you don't have a job? Why do you insist I take (or don't take) a job?

Just sometimes, solving the practical aspects of these issues alone is enough to resolve the conflict in your relationship: you start earning more money, and the arguments stop; your partner finds a job and suddenly there's no more fighting. The in-laws go home, and you start to feel able to have sex with each other again.

How can you tell if your problems can be sorted out so simply? Look at your rowing patterns. If you're normally able to sort your differences with a smile and a hug, but have suddenly found yourselves in the middle of full scale warfare over a single issue, then you probably fall into this category. You don't have a serious relationship conflict. You have a good track record in conflict management: it's just that this topic and this one alone that is a problem for you. If so, you may be able to solve your arguments right now just by putting your intelligence to work and coming up with practical solutions to the issues you face. Or, as you continue working through the steps, you may be able to use the skills you learn to find a workable resolution that suits you both; whether that's about spending the money, disciplining the children or sorting out the sex.

Almost always, however, the issue is a red herring. It's a symptom of your conflict rather than the cause. You're arguing because of much deeper-layer reasons. If these reasons are cleared, then the surface issue either never becomes a problem, or is easily resolved when it does.

BAD RELATIONSHIP DAYS

The next level down on the puzzle layers are lifestyle factors. Of course, when you're arguing it's your emotions that are important. But emotional vulnerability can stem from physical stress as well as mental strain. And such stress alone can be enough to trigger a fight. For example, you may be disagreeing about when to have sex. Now if you're resolving that while relaxing on a sunny beach in the middle of a week's holiday in Greece, the disagreement may be settled within seconds . . . If you're trying to resolve the issue at home, late at night after a few bottles of beer, when one of you is exhausted and the other needs to be up at six o'clock to start the early shift, things may turn out very differently.

Here are eight key elements in your life which can turn even the smallest and most trivial issue into a full-scale battle.

Tiredness

The current job market is incredibly insecure. And the consumer boom of recent years makes money seem vital. Both of these together mean that many people work at full capacity, to fulfil a budget commitment that is only just within their means. If you regularly fight in the evening or at the start of your weekends, consider swapping extended work hours and increased income for a more peaceful and loving relationship.

Stress

The pace of current life is hectic even if you're not physically exhausted. And you may feel you're not getting it right because you're not getting it all. This sort of tension can mean that you tend to hit out at your nearest and dearest whenever things are just too much for you. (Such stress can also mean you aren't motivated to have sex, a classic argument trigger.) Demanding less of yourself will mean that you can give more to your partnership. Ease back on the pressure; see if your local GP practice has a stress clinic; or buy one of the many books that teach you how to relax.

Alcohol

Drinking not only makes you more argumentative and aggressive; it also makes you less likely to worry about the fact that you're lashing out. The number of arguments in a partnership can rise in direct proportion to the number of units of alcohol you consume each evening. Particularly if you're prone to late-night quarrels, try not drinking completely for a month and see if that makes a difference.

Time apart

Conflict comes from disagreement that threatens. And if you don't spend enough quality time together, you can end up disagreeing

---

The number of arguments in a partnership rises in direct proportion to the number of units of alcohol consumed on Saturday night.

simply because you start to lose real contact with each other. If you fight more when you see each other less, take your diaries out. Build in a total of at least two hours' one-to-one talking time (no friends, no children, no television) every single week.

Special occasions

Some events quite simply trigger conflict. These may be celebrations – Christmas, holidays – or they may be demanding events, such as job interviews or the end of term. They may be 'sad memory events' when you're reminded of upsetting things that happened on this date: an accident, a miscarriage, a family death. Spot tricky occasions ahead of time and in the weeks before and after, be extra supportive to each other.

Lack of space

Rats kept in a very small cage end up eating each other. Humans trying to live in too small a space do much the same thing. If you don't have enough time alone, and don't have at least a small area you can call your own, you may well start fighting simply in order to carve out your own territory. If you think this may be the problem, try taking a short time apart each day, perhaps just after coming back from work. Even half an hour alone, or a solitary walk in the park, can help.

Illness

Someone who has been seriously ill is at a low ebb emotionally as well as physically. And illness depletes the energy of carers, too, particularly if they've had to be on call night and day. Both sides may also be coming to terms with the fact that life is not for ever. If there's been illness in your family, be prepared for a backlash – it has been known for patients suffering from severe 'flu to take a year to recover a sensibly optimistic view of life.

Hormones

Women in particular can suffer relationship earthquakes when their hormones are out of balance. Premenstrual tension can mean that one week out of four is an unhappy time. Pregnancy can mean that an entire nine months – plus a few more years of postnatal depression – are a sex free zone. The menopause can carve years out of a happy mid-life. And drugs that alter hormone balance, such as the contraceptive pill or anabolic steroids, can also tip the balance the wrong way, particularly if they make your sex drive plummet, which can feel worrying and threatening for both of you. If you think hormone changes may be underpinning your arguments, keep a diary charting your moods for about three months. Then take the evidence to a GP or alternative practitioner and demand help.

Each of these lifestyle factors has its own special, usually practical, solution. For all of them, you first need to admit there's a problem, and then do something about it. Most of these factors take time to sort out; they've taken months or years to affect you to the point that you end up fighting, so don't expect an overnight improvement. Give it time, and while you're waiting, go easy on each other. Accept that you're both on a short fuse, so shrug off irritability and unexpected tears. If a fight does start, knock it on the head as soon as possible and don't take it too seriously. All in all, remember that none of these factors truly concern your relationship. So be there for each other rather than against each other.

! ═══════════════ *Task 2.1* ═══════════════

Changing lifestyle

Consider the list of lifestyle factors that can affect your argument rate: tiredness, stress, alcohol, time apart, special occasions, lack of space, illness, hormones. How much do you think each affects you? Give each one a rating from 0 to 5, where 5 means that something affects you a lot, and 0 that it doesn't affect you at all.

    Think again about any factors to which you've given a 3, 4 or 5. What do you need in order to solve the problem: money? will-power? time? personal support? expert advice?

(Forward to Step 10, page 181**)**   **!**

WHOSE ARGUMENT ARE YOU HAVING?

Consider this. You may not actually be having your own argument. Even if the issue you're in conflict over seems to be entirely real and the antagonism very personal, it may be that others are influencing you. The next puzzle layer down may be the people in your life.

- Other people have relationship issues, and you play 'me too'. 'We left their house about 11.30 . . . by 11.35, on the dual carriageway, we were digging up resentments from well before we were married.' Being a witness to something often makes us want to join in. If you meet sniping friends, then you may start sniping too. (A variation on this is when the friends are so in love – or in lust – that it reminds you of how far you've drifted off course. Then you fight because of your dissatisfaction.)

- Other people stir up bad feelings in you, and you take it out on your partner: 'The boss really laid into me during the afternoon . . . When I arrived home I was still shaking . . . Fran called "Is that you?", and I just began yelling.' When you feel threatened and can't hit back – because the person is out of your reach physically, or because he or she is not someone you feel you can challenge, such as a work superior – it may feel a lot safer and easier to turn on someone who is close and available: your partner. This is particularly true if your children are acting up; you may reach the end of your tether with them, but then aim your frustration at your partner when the children are in bed.

- Other people stir up bad feelings in you, and your partner speaks for you: 'My sister keeps telling me I need to lose weight, but when Matt says she's wrong, I always end up saying she's right. He ends up asking whose side I'm on.' As a variation on the previous dynamic, when someone annoys you but you care too much to hit back, you may want your partner to act as ventriloquist's dummy. Your partner expresses your anger. You defend the person you're angry with. Then you replay with your partner the conversation you should be having with the person who annoyed you. Again, children are often involved here, with one of you speaking out against, and the other taking sides with, your offspring.

- Other people have a vested interest in your having problems, and so stir things up: 'My Mum's never liked Jordan . . . If she nags me about seeing him, I can guarantee that when I go round to his place that evening, we'll end up arguing.' Other people in your life may not want you to be a happy couple. They may dislike one of you. They may be jealous. They may be unhappy in their partnerships and want company in their misery. So they may stir up trouble for you.

In all these situations, the secret is to deal with the people directly rather than using your partner as a go-between or your relationship as a punch bag. Whose relationship is doing better than yours? Whose relationship problems are stirring up yours? Who has hurt you? Who is making trouble? Who is trying to come between you?

Instead of turning on each other, support each other to cope. If the issue is that you're comparing yourselves to another couple, then together use that as a motivation to improve your relationship. If the issue is that other people are coming between you, then together sort out a strategy to fend them off; helping each other to rehearse the lines that you want to say, then tackling the problem person and sorting out your issues with them. It's your relationship. Don't allow others to spoil it.

!━━━━━━━━━━ *Task 2.2* ━━━━━━━━━━

Hit list

Make a list of up to ten important people in your life. Then cross out the ones with whom you've never talked about your relationship at all, those who have never met you as a couple, those whose relationship you've never compared with your own.

For each of the ones left, complete the following sentence: 'I feel that . . . is influencing our relationship in these ways . . .'.

Do any of these people seem to be badly affecting the way you handle conflict in your relationship? If so, think about how you can stop him or her doing this.

It's vital to present a united front. So if you possibly can, talk with your partner about how to solve this one together. Remember: if it's not your argument, don't have it.

(Forward to Step 10, page 181**)** **!**

If it's not your argument, don't have it.

PAYOFFS YOU MAY NOT BE ABLE TO GIVE UP

Craig and Louisa argue all the time: in private, in public, in the car, in the supermarket. They challenge each other's beliefs. They question each other's motives. And, they pull no punches: 'Everyone was laughing at you, you were so stupid!' They take every aspect of each other's behaviour and tear it to pieces, savagely.

But do Craig and Louisa want to stop arguing? Do they feel the need to alter their relationship? Absolutely not. They've been together for nearly a decade, and if offered a magic cure for their constant fights, both would refuse it. For Craig and Louisa, arguing has become a way of life. It's certainly painful. But through it, they have excitement, intensity, intimacy; things they don't find any other way. They live on an emotional roller-coaster, always challenging each other, always being challenged. In all honesty, even if they tried to shift their conflict patterns, they probably wouldn't succeed. For all the downsides, they'll probably stick with what they have, because of all the other payoffs.

Payoffs that may mean you don't want to give up fighting:

- *Excitement:* when you fight, the adrenaline pours and your heart rate speeds. It's as good as sex, and often leads to love-making.
- *Intimate communication:* being angry is the only time you express your real feelings or needs. Fighting is the only time you communicate. If you didn't argue, you wouldn't truly know each other.
- *Distance:* regular fighting is a way to maintain some emotional distance. And if you're ever feeling particularly trapped or claustrophobic, there's an easy way out. Start an argument. This is particularly true in bed, when starting a fight may be the way to avoid having sex altogether when you simply don't have the energy or the inclination.
- *Love:* you only feel truly loved when you're arguing, possibly because you confuse the strong emotion that you feel when you're fighting, with the strong emotions of 'in love'.

- *Attention:* starting a fight is the only way to capture your partner's attention. Even if only for a few moments, you're the centre of his or her world.
- *Security:* by risking your relationship through an argument, you test it out. If the relationship survives, you feel secure. Of course, you can never be sure that the partnership is completely stable, so you always have to have just one more fight.
- *Contraception:* in some relationships, fighting raises desire. For you it lowers desire. So if your partner starts to make a move, and you aren't 'in the mood', you pick a fight.
- *Stability:* when everything's fine, you sometimes feel guilty or nervous that you're just so happy. By spoiling all that, a fight keeps the comfortable if unsatisfactory status quo.

Stopping arguments when the payoffs are so deep-rooted can be as difficult as trying to write with your left hand when you're naturally right-handed. For if the bottom line is that the only way to have intimacy, excitement and fulfilment in your relationship is to argue, then you'll carry on arguing.

Of course, good conflict management doesn't mean never having a cross word or never raising your voice. Particularly if you need to express your emotion or some deep needs, a short, sharp yell at your partner may be an excellent way to begin that process. But if fighting is the only way you can communicate or show your love, then however good it feels in the short term, painful arguments won't work long term. Unless you're solving the issues elsewhere, then long term your dissatisfaction with your relationship will rise, and your joy in it will fall.

If the only way to have intimacy, excitement and fulfilment in your relationship is to argue, then you'll carry on arguing.

As you learn more about conflict management, you'll learn a good deal about gaining the skills to meet your needs. As you master them, use these skills to make sure that you don't have to argue in order to have what you want from your relationship.

!——————————— *Task 2.3* ———————————

Payoffs

If you know that arguing meets needs that otherwise wouldn't be met, then ask yourself how you can have these needs met elsewhere. Which of the following payoffs do you gain from arguments? For each one you notice, consider ways in which you could have your needs met without having to argue.

In the list below, the first type of need – attention – has example payoffs already worked out. Consider the idea of attention for yourself, and then think about the same issues for each of the other needs below.

Need	How arguments meet the need	Other ways to meet the need
Attention	eg: When we fight I know he's concentrating on me	eg: I could arrange for us to go out for one-on-one meals more rather than having to share him with the television every evening.
Excitement		
Intimacy		
Distance		
Love		
Security		
Contraception		
Stability		

(Forward to Step 10, page 181**)**   !

———————NOT JUST HERE AND NOW———————

Your fights may well not be because of what's happening right now. On the next puzzle layer down, the reasons for your fight may lie in the past rather than the present.

The past has made you who you are. Your early childhood, your adolescence, your adult years have all formed you. Everyone you've known – parents, family, teachers, friends, religious leaders, past partners – have all taught you how to think, how to feel, how to behave.

In particular, you've learned about love and about sex. When you saw your parents cuddling on the sofa, watched your friends giggling behind the bike sheds, listened to your friends talking about their latest conquests, or lost your virginity in the back of a car, you kept on adding to your impression of what partnerships are about. You learned what people do when they fall in love, when they commit to each other, when they form a stable relationship. You learned how couples make love together, work together, run a house, have children.

Your picture of how partnerships should be feels absolutely, undeniably true. You believe in it as the way the world is. Moreover, you believe in it as the way the world should be, as 'life rules'. So if your parents hardly ever talked, then you'll grow up believing that silent partnerships are the norm. If your image of marriage is that 'she should' stay at home and 'he should' go to work, you'll see that as absolutely natural. You may not like these 'rules'. You may rebel against them and try to run your relationships in a totally opposite way. But you treat the rules as if they were common to everyone, a deep-rooted tacit agreement. You often live your life completely unaware that there is any difference between the way you think relationships should be run, and what other people think should happen.

All this forms the next layer of reasons why you argue. For, happily, all of us are different. And that means that we all have very different rules which we follow or discard. Of course, we begin our relationships convinced that the person we've chosen will follow our rules. But when our differences start to show through, we disagree. If you think relationships should be lived out in companionable silence, then fall in love with someone who wants a relationship where you both talk all the time, you'll feel uneasy. (Or, if you rebelled against silent partnerships and want constant chat, you'll hate it if your partner wants even a moment's quiet.) Here comes the conflict.

'Chantelle was French, I was English. We met on holiday, phoned each other every day, were married by Christmas. Then, the problems started. I'd been brought up to believe that a husband looks after his wife: my mum has never worked because she was so busy

bringing up me and my brother and sisters. My dad had always brought in enough money. But Chantelle loved her job and saw no reason why she shouldn't carry on in England. When I tried to convince her that she could stay at home, she felt trapped and bored. When she went for interviews, I saw it as her way of saying she didn't think I could support her. We argued for six months solid about it. And then she went back to France.'   Michael

Particularly nowadays, at the turn of the millennium, there's a great deal of conflict over relationship life rules. For not only are people's backgrounds very different: fifty years ago, you'd have expected to marry someone from your area and with your background and culture, while nowadays it's very possible that, like Chantelle and Michael, you'll marry someone from another area, another culture, another background.

Also the social changes of the last half century – women going to work, high unemployment, low birth rate – have meant that gender roles in particular are always shifting. And the changes in our attitudes to sex – the contraceptive pill, sex before marriage, multiple partners – have meant that our expectations of what happens in a sexual relationship are also in flux.

The result is that even people with a common culture, even people from the same family, may have completely differing life rules about what should happen in a relationship. If this happens to you, you may not only differ and feel bad about that; you may believe that if your partner is different, or approaches things differently, he or she is doing it deliberately. You may believe that if your partner doesn't instinctively know what you expect and need, then they are failing in their love for you.

The way to begin to tackle this issue, and to stop it creating painful arguments, is to realise that the differences between you and your partner are completely normal and natural. You feel annoyed at your partner because he or she sees things one way. Your partner feels annoyed at you because you do things another way. In fact, you and your life rules are individual and wonderfully unique. For you to both be the same – or even know ahead of time what the other wants and expects – is like sending a rocket to the moon. It's been done, but it's not the easiest or most common of developments.

What you can do is to start swapping notes. Make sure you both know about each other's life rules. For if you're aware of the differences between you, then you'll find them more bearable because they're not an unexpected shock. You'll find them less threatening because you understand that they come from the past. You'll start to understand and appreciate each of your particular reasons for thinking and feeling as you do, and this may mean that you can actually start celebrating differences, be proud of your own ways of doing things, and admire your partner's ways. Also, you can begin to do what Michael and Chantelle couldn't: to negotiate practical ways of behaving, ways that bridge the gaps between you.

! ============== *Task 2.4* ==============

Lessons from the past

Complete these sentences. Then think what they tell you about the way you think relationships have to be.

Love is . . .
A good (female) partner or wife is . . .
A good (male) partner or husband is . . .
A good sexual relationship has to include . . .
The most important thing in a partnership is . . .
The most awful betrayal in a partnership would be . . .

If you can swap notes with your partner, then compare your different views. If you can't swap notes with your partner then use your own awareness to make notes about his or her views.

Which differences between your respective views are currently adding to the conflict in your relationship?

What could you do to be more tolerant of the differences between you?

(Forward to Step 10, page 181) !

WHEN THE RULES CHANGE

Sometimes, your individual differences aren't a problem. Sometimes your life rules don't differ at all, or not very much. Or, your differences create strength and compatibility; and continue to do that. Sometimes, you're able to resolve your differences by under-standing, flexibility, straight talking and compromise. Whether you're deciding on how many children to have, or what colour the lounge carpet should be, the gaps are easily bridgeable.

But then, into your secure life, comes a change. And that disturbs everything. This is the next puzzle layer.

'We met and fell in love when we were both at FE college, both young, both poor. We moved in together within two months, helped each other with our assignments, turned vegetarian to save money, thought and felt exactly the same. Until four years ago, when we left college. I started working in a home for old people, which I love. Hayley started a job as a PA, which she loves. But it's all been a big mistake for the relationship. She works all the hours of the day because her boss is something big in the City. When she comes home, I want to talk about what my grannies have been up to, and she's either not interested or too tired to listen. She expects me to be grateful that she's bringing the money in. I'd just be grateful if she was interested in me. We don't argue any more now, just avoid each other.' Glen

Something changed for Glen and Hayley. Over the course of their lives, they'd gathered all kinds of life rules about what to do as a student, and what to do as a worker. When they met, as students, their life rules were compatible — and so were they. But when their jobs created a very different situation from the one in which they met, the rules shifted and so did their compatiblity.

The rules that they used as students were different from the ones they used as workers. Life altered. They moved on. Each of them changed the rules.

But, they didn't tell each other. Glen had no idea that Hayley would want to work so hard, and ask him to help her to do so. Hayley didn't realise that once Glen was on the sharp end of the caring services, he would expect more emotional support. The resentment they felt at these new demands, this 'rule changing', was what made their fights so bitter.

Shifts in life are inevitable. And when life shifts, and it shifts you, then it will shift your relationship. Then, however well you both related in the past, and however compatible your life rules have been up to now, expect fireworks.

Here are six key life changes that may mean that you change the rules on each other.

- *Commitment:* you shift from 'going out' to 'engaged . . . living together . . . married'.

  You may each expect different things from a spouse than from someone who is just a boyfriend or girlfriend. You need to negotiate issues such as loyalty, fidelity and who does the housework. You may particularly tend to fight about how you should behave now you're a couple.

- *Childrearing:* the baby arrives and suddenly there's three.

  He may still want couple intimacy, but it's less possible. She may now expect practical help with the childrearing, which he doesn't realise is necessary. The two of you may particularly tend to fight about division of labour. And because having a baby often leads to a dramatic drop in the amount you have sex, there may be a shift away from the physical side of your relationship, which may dismay or anger you.

- *Career shift:* you go back to work, gain promotion, undergo a job change, be made redundant.

  Practical expectations may alter – who does the housework, who pays the bills? But expectations of who has control in the relationship may shift too. Who makes the key decisions now that she's earning a salary, or he's redundant? You may particularly tend to fight about practicalities.

- *Empty-nest syndrome:* the children leave home.

  Often, you each have totally different expectations of what will happen now: for her to take a job, for both of you to spend more time together. A totally separate pressure may be that you've forgotten how to relate to each other as a couple rather than talking 'through the children'. You particularly tend to fight about one of you wanting to 'break away'.

- *Reaching a plateau:* you realise that you've achieved most of what you're going to.

  When one or both of you finally realises that in career, looks or money, life is now on a downhill slide, you may panic. You particularly tend to fight about one of you acting 'too old' or 'too young'. One of you may, for example, feel that as far as sex is concerned you're over the hill, or want reassurance that you're still desirable.

- *Retirement:* you pull back from the world.
  Intimations of mortality change everything. You both need to adapt to a life where, increasingly, illness and frailty are part of the deal. You particularly fight about disillusionment. Was it actually worthwhile devoting a lifetime to your relationship? If it wasn't, whose fault is that?

How can you cope? Part of the secret is simply having practical and emotional support: life nowadays is so frenetic that any further stress caused by a change will increase your emotional vulnerability and so leave you more likely to spiral into conflict. Slow down. Take things more easily. Ask friends and family to help. If necessary, pull back from too much change. The couple who scheduled a job move, a house move and a new baby in the first three months of the year were simply asking for trouble.

But the most important task is to update each other on who you are, now life has shifted. If you're arguing, it's probably because you have new expectations and haven't realigned them. So do that. Specifically, use what you learn in later sections of this book to develop your ability to talk about how your life rules have changed. Swap notes on what new rules you're developing, and what is new about what you need and expect from each other. Then keep pace with each others' changes, and change along with each other. An alteration in your partner's world view isn't necessarily a threat. In fact, it may be a promise of better things to come. For life change can resolve conflict rather than create it. If, in making any of these shifts, your individual rules become more similar than your old ones, then you may actually relate better than before.

Carl and Adrienne were fighters to the death before they had their baby, Claire. However, they found that once she arrived, not only were they in total agreement about how to behave as parents, but also, when faced with the important and time-consuming job of bringing Claire up, they simply buckled to as a team and settled their disagreements rather than wrangling over them. That's not to fall into the trap of thinking that a life change will save a failing relationship. It won't. But it can positively realign a partnership that's basically sound.

Keep pace with each others' changes, and change along with each other.

!======================= *Task 2.5* =======================

Lifeline

On a piece of paper, draw a horizontal line to represent your relationship until now. At the left-hand end of the line, mark the year you met. At the right-hand end of the line, put the present year. Mark on the line any key points: moving in together, wedding day, children's birth dates, etc.

Now mark in any life changes you've been through. When did they happen? How long did they last? How did they affect your relationship: your love life, your sex life? Are they still affecting your relationship now?

If you've just begun a life stage, think about that too. How have your feelings changed? Do you expect different things of each other now that you're in this life stage, in terms of what you do, say, feel; particularly in terms of communication, division of labour and sexuality? Is that causing disagreements?

If you can swap notes with your partner, talk though your thoughts.

What could you be doing to offset the problems that life changes are causing in your relationship?

(Forward to Step 10, page 181**)**   **!**

___THE THREE FUNDAMENTAL NEEDS___

'We'd been together for about six months when we started arguing about the shopping. Every week, we'd have a fight on Thursday about who was going to go to the supermarket on Friday. Then on Friday night, we'd have a fight about whether whoever had done the shopping had bought the right things. When we'd been doing this for ten weeks running, we stopped and asked what was going on.

'We realised that the real issue wasn't the shopping. It was our relationship. We'd agreed that we'd start trying for a baby at Christmas. And I'd started feeling out of control, as if once I was pregnant, I'd be completely dependent on Alan. I needed to know that he was willing to consider what I wanted – even in something as small as the shopping – to show he loved me and cared for me. Then I could trust that he would love and care for me and be willing

*to take my needs into account even once I had the baby and was
"stuck". The answer's been to hold back on the "baby plan" until we
know each other more. I need to know that he's really committed
when we eventually do become parents.'* Laura

Whatever your surface issue is, it may mask a much deeper level
of problem. And this is the next layer of the puzzle.

All the key areas of argument – such as money, children,
family, sex, work – are areas where people have much deeper
needs. If you're arguing about money, it's often not the hard cash
that's the issue, but how much each partner is 'worth' in the
relationship. If you're arguing about the kids, that often hides a
worry about whether you're really getting it right as parents.

Arguments about sex in particular are often not about the
nitty-gritty of what happens in bed, but the deeper needs that are
expressed during love-making. Sex is often a metaphor, a symbol
of love. So if you're arguing about not making love as much as
you used to, the real concern may be whether you care about each
other as much as you used to. Or if the fight is about one of you
demanding something particular in bed, then the deeper issue
may well be about who's demanding what outside the bedroom.
Sex and love are so intertwined that arguments about sex are
almost always arguments about love.

Do you find you start with one such issue and move swiftly on
to several others during a single argument? Do you sort out your
issues on a practical level but still not feel satisfied? Do you
contact strong feelings as the two of you discuss surface matters?
If so, you're probably dealing with deeper layers of need. These
may be many and varied – security, respect, fidelity, loyalty,
fulfilment, affection – and, of course, love. One way to look at it,
though, is as three broad areas, three Fundamental Needs: feeling
valued, feeling in control, and feeling successful.

Worth: you need to feel valued

Does my partner value me? Does the fact that he sides with his
mother mean that I'm less important to him than she is? Does the
fact that he expects me to do the housework as well as hold down
a job mean that he feels that the job I do is less worthwhile than
the job he does? Does the fact that he always takes his climax, but

doesn't worry about whether I've had mine, mean that my desires aren't important to him?

You may be arguing about the surface issues, but what you actually need is to be reassured that you and your individuality are worthwhile and that your partner knows it. You may express this in a number of ways: you want respect, you want to be cherished, you want to be taken seriously, you want to be loved. When you fight, it's because you believe that by doing that, you can force your partner to value you.

Control: you need to feel in charge

What's the power balance between us? Does the fact that my partner earns more than I do mean he feels he has power over me? Does the fact that she doesn't sleep with me any more mean that I'm losing control of the situation?

When you fight with your partner, often what lies underneath is a power struggle, over who makes the decisions in your relationship and who determines what happens. All human beings need to feel that they have control in their lives. In a partnership, that usually means needing to know that you at least have equal say in what happens. If you're suffering from long-term conflict you may even feel that the safest thing would be to be in total control. You use defence and attack to try to get this complete power.

Success: you need to feel you're not a failure

Am I a good partner? Does the fact that our children are acting up mean that I'm a bad parent? Does the fact that we argue so much mean that our relationship is doomed long term?

When you feel you're failing, or that your partner thinks you're failing, you end up feeling insecure and unhappy. And in a destructive twist, the way you try to re-establish your security and happiness is to try to win in conflict. Whatever your failures in other areas of your life, if you beat your partner in an argument or score a point in a debate, then short term you feel as if you are succeeding.

If you suspect that underneath the surface of your conflict lie deeper agendas, then you have to sort out more than just the practicalities. You have to think carefully about what you need.

And then you have to find out what to do in order to meet those needs. Make a start by considering what possible agendas may be lurking under the surface of your arguments.

! ========================= *Task 2.6* =========================

Going deeper

Is there a main issue that you're arguing about at the moment? If there is, take a piece of paper and write a single word that represents the issue at the top of the paper.

Underneath that, draw a line from top to bottom of the paper, dividing it into two halves. In one half, write down the deeper issues that concern you: perhaps concerns about your relationship or worries about the future. In the other half of the paper, write down the deeper issues that concern your partner (if you can't swap notes with each other, write down the issues that you think concern your partner.) Particularly mention any Fundamental Needs that you feel aren't being met.

At the bottom of the page, write down what you could do in order to make a start in solving these issues.

(Forward to Step 10, page 181)

!

___ ___ EMOTIONAL TIME BOMBS___ ___

Right at the heart of the puzzle lie the most powerful reasons why you may be arguing: past betrayals. Everyone suffers such betrayals during their life. Perhaps yours happened recently or perhaps many years before. Perhaps it was from your parents, friends or an early partner. Perhaps it involved a tiny and unmemorable, or an important and extremely traumatic, incident. Whoever and whenever, your sense of betrayal has stayed with you, an emotional time bomb that will explode in your life if anything similar ever seems to be happening again.

If it does seem to be happening again – in even the smallest of ways – then the bomb starts to tick. And unfortunately, it ticks underneath the person who matters most to you: your partner. Even if what originally happened had nothing to do with him or her, you need to make sure that, of all people, your partner doesn't repeat your past unhappiness.

When she was six years old, Diane's dad and mum parted when her mum met someone else. Feeling that Diane would become confused and upset between 'two fathers', her dad chose not to keep in touch, and she hasn't seen him since. Now, thirty years later, every time her husband Roy, a long-distance lorry driver, goes away, they fight. Diane knows that he has to leave, for his job. And she has the children for company. But all that doesn't stop her feeling panic-stricken fury every time he goes: rage which she first felt as a six-year-old, seeing her dad wave goodbye for the last time.

You may not be aware what the betrayal is. You may not know what's affecting how you feel. You may not know what you're emotional about: it may be too far back in your memory. If an emotion seems overwhelming, and much bigger than the issues, you're almost certainly remembering an earlier betrayal. You're almost certainly sensing an emotional time bomb.

It may seem as if such bombs can't be handled. How can you come to terms with something that happened years ago? How can you defuse such strong feelings?

It helps if you can recognise what is happening. It particularly helps if you can start to tell the difference between what was happening then and what is happening now. If you can understand that the fear you feel when your partner walks out of the door – or doesn't phone you, or doesn't have sex with you – is actually the panic that first started when your dad walked out, then you'll immediately be at an advantage. Armed with this information, you can begin to recognise that the situations are different, the people are different, and you are different. You'll be able to cope much more easily with what's happening.

WHERE ARE YOU NOW?

Step 2 has helped you understand what may be causing your arguments, and start working on the more obvious and easily resolvable causes. (You can begin to resolve the deeper causes in later steps.)

As you complete the tasks in this step, remember to turn to Step 10 on page 180–181 and fill in the relevant sections there.

Move on to Step 3 when:

- you feel you've understood that painful arguments happen for lots of reasons, not just the 'issues' that you're arguing about.

- you've checked out and taken action on the 'surface' causes of your arguments.

- you've started to identify the deeper causes and, if possible, have swapped notes with each other on what these might be.

ANALYSE HOW YOU ARE ARGUING

'We'd been sleeping together for about two weeks, and it was fine. By fine, I mean that it was cuddly and arousing and nice. But I never climaxed. And about the sixth time we were in bed, it suddenly dawned on me that I wasn't going to climax, and that he hadn't even registered the fact. I rolled away from him – right in the middle of it – and I felt this total fury, from all the times I'd been in bed with someone and it hadn't even crossed their mind to check out what was going on for me. He didn't know what was happening. He stuttered "Are you OK?" I got out of bed, picked up my clothes, got dressed, left. I feel ashamed now: it wasn't all his fault, and I could at least have explained. But at the time, the only way I could handle my fury was to run.' Christine

When you're in the middle of relationship conflict, you haven't time to stop and think. You're sticking up for your rights. You're fending off aggression. And it can often seem as if you are, quite literally, fighting for survival; emotional if not physical.

So you never stop to analyse what's happening. You never stop to think 'Where does that come from? Why am I acting this way? When I do that, what does my partner do, and vice versa?' It can be easy to forget that the way you handle conflict may not be the only way. You feel you're acting spontaneously, in the only way you can, by sheer instinct.

In fact, the way you handle conflict isn't spontaneous and natural. It's a well-learned and carefully honed product of your background, your upbringing, your personality, and a great deal of 'on-the-job' training. Throughout your life, you've learned how to fight in the same way as you've learned how to walk and talk.

Analysing the way you argue – and realising where all the bits come from – is a vital part of resolving your conflict patterns. For if you're able to understand that you've simply borrowed your fighting patterns from people in your past, then you can choose to give them back. If you're able to realise just what you're doing when you fight, then you can choose, quite simply, not to do it any more. To break the pattern or kick the habit of your arguments, you have to analyse how you're arguing.

CONFLICT IN YOUR CRADLE

The most basic lessons you learn about handling conflict begin when you're a few hours old. For you need to survive. And in order to survive, you need to have some kind of way of meeting your needs. If a newborn baby doesn't have its needs met sufficiently to keep warm, fed and dry, then it dies. If a toddler doesn't have its needs met sufficiently to be paid attention, cuddled and talked to, then it never develops to be human.

At first, you motivate people do what you want by crying. At a few months old, you learn to smile in order to persuade adults to care for you. Later still, you learn to talk, snuggle, point and snatch: in fact, to use all your verbal and non-verbal skills to obtain what you need. And what do you need? On a survival level, maybe food, drink and a cuddle. On a more subtle level, all kinds of underlying needs, such as knowing you're loved, being in control of your life, getting it right.

You have two problems in meeting your needs. The first is that what you as an individual child want is different to what those around you want. Quite rightly, the grown-ups reckon that you can't always be the centre of the universe, that there are other people around who have needs too. You meet your first disagreement, your first taste of conflict.

The second problem is that you often aren't sure that you're up to this conflict. You're smaller than everyone around you, the adults have more decision-making power than you do, and you're often given the message that somehow you're failing. You enter any battle hampered by the fear that you might not win.

So when you go for what you want – to be the centre of attention, to come first in the race, to leave the Brussels sprouts on your plate – you do so with very mixed feelings. You're defensive because you feel vulnerable. You're aggressive because you fear you can't have what you want. The result is that you try different ways to win the battle, and while some of them are helpful, others actually aren't. You're not being deliberately naughty. You're just doing what comes naturally.

Here are some of the ways children cope with conflict between themselves and the world around them. Do any feel familiar to you?

Child thinks . . .	Child does . . .
If I'm good enough, I'll have what I want.	Is quiet, submissive, smiling, 'good', 'I love you, Daddy.'
If I hold on, they can't abandon me.	Clingy, insecure, 'Don't go.'
If I fight them off early enough, they won't hurt me.	Spiky, defensive, nervous, edgy, critical, 'Don't' . . . 'Go away.'
If I don't give in to them, they'll give in to me.	Digging heels in, saying 'won't, shan't, don't want to'.
If I make enough noise, then I'll have what I want.	Screaming, hitting, biting, scratching, 'I'll cry and cry until I'm sick.'
If I persuade them enough, they'll see reason.	Debating, 'Why?. . . Why not?. . . You said . . .'
If I act needy enough, then they'll give me what I want.	Whining, whinging, 'pleeeeease'
If I don't do it with a smile, then I'm not really giving in.	Sulking, sullen, 'I'm only doing it because you told me to.'
If I reject them, then they'll do what I want.	Pushing away, turning away, sulking, 'I don't love you any more.'
If I can't have something openly, then I'll be underhand.	. Telling lies, playing off parents against each other, 'Emma's got one. Why can't I have one?'
If I can't control the world, at least I can control my feelings.	Withdrawing, going very still and quiet, 'I just want to be on my own.'
I can trust myself and the world to have what I want.	Saying what they want, accepting when they can't have it, 'OK, you have the first turn now and I'll go first tomorrow.'

You probably started off doing all these things when you were very young. You found that some gained you what you wanted and others didn't. You did more of the ones that worked, and less of the ones that didn't work. Growing up, you specialised into some ways of handling disagreement, and let the others go. Your adult conflict patterns were already being formed.

LESSONS FROM MUM AND DAD

'I think I have the worst of both worlds: my father's world and my mother's world. She was brought up in the war years, and was like a brick wall. She never broke down, never showed that anything upset her. He'd seen active service, but couldn't cope with the world, knuckled under to everything. If they argued, he'd splutter and shout, make a terrible noise. She'd just sit there and listen, but she always got her own way in the end. What I do is I shout and splutter, but I also dig my heels in. I've made both my wives give in; otherwise they never had any peace. Well, maybe I'm not as bad as that. But I do hear my father and my mother every time I open my mouth.'   Stephen

The next lessons you learn come from what you see around you. For as mentioned in Step 2, as children all of us watch, listen, and develop 'life rules' about the way the world operates. Crucially, as we grow, we develop rules of how conflict should be managed. Mainly, we learn our conflict rules from our parent figures, those most important people in our lives, who teach us directly by how they cope with disagreement.

Sometimes, parents cope well. They disagree, and make it clear that's no big deal. They act as if conflict can be resolved. They show us how to do that resolving. So when Dad wants to chop down the big hedge in the garden, and Mum wants to keep it because she likes the shade, they talk about it. They sort out a solution, they act on it. We watch, listen, and copy their technique.

Often, though, parents cope badly. They teach us how not to handle conflict. They act out for us, in front of our impressionable eyes, just how to behave if we want to hurt our partner. Or, particularly if the conflict trigger is something they're uncomfortable about, such as sex, they hide things away, so we never even realise that conflicts happen and have to be handled. Here are ten of the things that our parents teach us. Do any strike a chord with you?

- 'Put up and shut up.' (Either do something to solve a problem or don't complain about it.)
- 'Love conquers all.' (If you sacrifice enough, then you'll overcome all difficulties.)
- 'Never apologise, never explain.' (Do what you want; don't be accountable to anyone else.)
- 'Don't be a doormat.' (If you let your partner get away with it, they'll trample all over you.)
- 'Don't get mad, get even.' (Anger achieves nothing; strategic exploitation works better.)
- 'Keep your partner under your thumb.' (The best way to run a relationship is with you firmly in charge.)
- 'Just twist him round your little finger.' (Behind-the-scenes manipulation is the best way forward, particularly for women.)
- 'Guess who wears the trousers in their house?' (Men should say what happens in a relationship. If a woman does, then there's something wrong.)
- 'Not in front of the children.' (Arguing is so awful that it simply shouldn't be done in public.)
- 'Don't let your guard down.' (People will take advantage of you if you show your emotions.)

Typically, as you grow, you tend to learn the conflict styles used by one of your parents. It's often the same gender parent, but not always. You may also combine bits of both parents' ways of fighting, resulting in a lethal cocktail of unhelpful behaviours. A more unusual variation is to decide never ever to copy your parents, so if they pushed everything under the carpet, you fight loudly and with fervour, and if they woke the neighbours you never raise your voice. Whichever way you jump, your parents' ways of handling conflict add yet more options to how you fight.

YOUR TURN TO FIGHT

You don't only learn about conflict from your parents. You learn about conflict 'on the job'. As you grow up, and your needs clash with those of others, you learn what to do simply by having to cope.

You begin with your brothers, sisters and friends. These 'equals' are the first people you can actively fight with because unlike your parents, they aren't in charge of you. So you may learn to stand up for your own individuality, fight clean, and come to a fair settlement. On the other hand, if you're the eldest in your family or your class, always being told to 'look after the little ones', then in conflict, you may need to have total control. If you're the youngest on your block, you may be bullied or babied and turn out unable to stand up for your own rights or unable to ever give anyone else theirs. If you are piggy-in-the-middle, you'll probably learn early how to negotiate – or to manipulate. As Gary commented, 'I hate it when my wife stops me doing anything. My elder sister sat on me when I was little, and it's exactly the same feeling!'

As you grow older, learning to be adult involves learning to make your own decisions and put them into practice. And often, this means learning to stand up for yourself against authority figures, general and specific. If your parents tell you to be in by ten, and you want to stay out until midnight, then you're in conflict. Now, you may learn to negotiate solutions that broadly suit everyone: you're in by ten except on Saturdays. But if you stay out late every night and get away with it, then you may end up labouring under the delusion that you can have whatever you want. Or, you may be dominated into aways being home by ten, in which case you may rebel, or learn that giving in to other people is the only safe move.

Esther, who was never able to stand up to her husband, commented that throughout her teens, her father never let her have the last word in an argument. 'I remember for my eighteenth birthday, he asked me what I wanted as a present. I told him exactly: a silver ring, a present from him to me. He didn't even blink before saying, "No, that wouldn't be suitable. You'll be married within a few years and then you'll be wearing gold". I thought: "Fine. I'll just keep my mouth shut in future."'

Finally, you learn to handle partnership conflict directly. You fall in love. You try out your conflict patterns with each partner, and learn new lessons, by the way they react. But this time, there's a twist. You're not dealing with little sisters or school bullies, opponents or authority figures. You're trying to resolve conflict with someone you actively want to have a working relationship with, someone whose happiness is important to you, someone you hope will love you, admire you, care for you, have sex with you. It's not so easy to simply go for victory.

If you're already skilled in conflict management, and lucky enough to find a similarly skilled partner, you may be one of the very few couples who cope wonderfully with all disagreements. You'll fight rarely, and you'll meet your own needs and those of your partner most of the time.

If not, then the intensity of love and lust may teach you some unhelpful lessons. You may learn to give in when your partner wants to go to a particular film. You may learn to sulk if that strategy seems to persuade your partner to have sex with you. You may learn to lose confidence and simply withdraw whenever an argument looms. And then you may end up facing each new partnership in the desperate hope that, this time, it will be all right. The problem becomes that to each new relationship, you bring even more fear, even more anger.

!————————— *Task 3.1* —————————

Conflict school

What lessons were you taught about conflict by people in your past?
  Complete these sentences.

My parents taught me ...
My brothers and sisters taught me ...
My friends taught me ...
My teachers taught me ...
The leaders in my community taught me ...
My earlier partners taught me ...

Now underline any of these lessons that you think aren't useful to you in your present relationship and that you think you'd like to stop using now.

(Forward to Step 10, page 181)   **!**

__WHAT ARE YOUR CONFLICT STYLES?__

Over the years, then, you've had a lot of training in how to fight. And from it, you've developed your own methods of arguing.

But though personalised, that method is made up of basic building blocks, conflict styles that most people use. You'll mix and match them. You'll use different approaches, according to what your partner does, how you feel, what the issue is. You'll develop your method over the years, as relationship follows relationship.

Read on, through these building blocks, these conflict styles. Start noticing which you use, and how often. Notice too that many of them come directly from what you learned, even as a baby, from your parents, from your 'on-the-job' practice. For example, if when young you tended to be obedient rather than defiant, and you saw one of your parents behaving in a similar way with your other parent, then when push comes to shove, you'll probably use the 'appeasement' style. If you often hit out, and then found that in the playground fisticuffs gained you what you wanted, then lo and behold, you'll be tempted to use 'high-level attack'.

Appeasement

Inside, she feels: 'I'm not worth anything . . . he'll reject me.'

In partnership conflict she may:

. . . give in, agree, apologise; even if her partner is trampling all over her: 'Of course we'll do it your way. . . sorry I even mentioned it.'

. . . justify her behaviour by telling herself: 'If I give him everything he wants, then he'll love me. If I make trouble, he'll leave.'

. . . cling emotionally or literally, be possessive or jealous: 'You do love me, don't you?'

. . . justify her behaviour by telling herself: 'If I show him how much I need him, then he'll have to love me.'

Pre-emptive strike

Inside, he feels: 'Life's so tricky . . . if I don't watch it, I'll be hurt.'

In partnership conflict he may:

... think his partner is attacking him whatever the evidence: 'Just don't start, that's all.'

... justify his behaviour by telling himself: 'I need to spot trouble before it starts.'

... dig his heels in on any issue; simply not play ball: 'Sorry, it's out of the question.'

... justify his behaviour by telling himself: 'If I give an inch, she'll take a mile.'

... always say how things should be: 'You mustn't . . .' 'You shouldn't . . .'

... justify his behaviour by telling himself: 'Unless I lay down the rules, this relationship will get totally out of order.'

... up the ante immediately trouble starts; threatens to leave; leaves: 'That's it. No more.'

... justify his behaviour by telling himself: 'I have to make a stand or she won't realise how serious this is.'

High-level attack

Inside, he feels: 'The world's such a dangerous place. I need to fight for my rights.'

In partnership conflict he may:

... simply attack: tell partner straight out all his critical feelings, have hysterics, use verbal and sometimes physical violence: 'How dare you . . . don't do that!'

... justify his behaviour by telling himself: 'There's no point in being reasonable; fighting's the only way to survive!'

Low-level attack

Inside, she feels: 'If I go for what I want head-on, there'll be trouble. I need to play it carefully.'

In partnership conflict she may:

... use argument to win the day: 'But what you want just isn't logical . . . reasonable . . . sensible.'

... justify her behaviour by telling herself: 'I'm being reasonable, but he just won't listen.'

... nag, whinge, use emotional blackmail: 'Why aren't you as good in bed as . . . . It's three weeks since I asked you to . . .'

... justify her behaviour by telling herself: 'If I didn't keep on at him, I'd never have what I want.'

... go along with things but very unwillingly: 'Look, I'm doing what you wanted, OK?'

... justify her behaviour by telling herself: 'My knuckling under isn't a failure if I do it under duress.'

... sulk, cut off, use silence to punish: 'You should know what you've done.'

... justify her behaviour by telling herself: 'This'll show him he can't do without me.'

... be nice as pie, but secretly work to obtain what she wants: 'I personally agree with you, but you never know what people might think.'

... justify her behaviour by telling herself: 'Being sneaky is the only way to get what I want.'

Retreat

Inside, he feels: 'I can't take the strain; from others, and from my own feelings.'

In partnership conflict, he may:

... withdraw, put up a wall of silence, not interact, refuse to admit there's a problem, walk out: 'The only problem is that you're emotional.'

... justify his behaviour by telling himself: 'I'm not sinking to this level.'

Win-win

She feels: 'I'm all right, and so are other people. There's no need for either of us to lose. We can both win.'

In partnership conflict she may:

... outline what she wants, listen to other people's needs, talk flexibly about solutions, go for it: 'Let's talk ... I need ... what do you need?. . . I understand you. Are we both happy now?'

... justify her behaviour by telling herself: 'In my experience, things work better when we both have what we want.'

! ================= *Task 3.2* =================

Personal styles

Go back through the descriptions of individual conflict styles. Tick or underline any things that you do . . . say . . . think.

Then add up the number of ticks for each style. Do you largely use one style or a mixture?

Go back through the descriptions again with a different coloured pen. Tick or underline any things you've seen or heard your partner do during arguments. Then add up the number of ticks in each style. Does your partner largely use one style or a mixture?

Think of what you'd like to change about the styles you use when you argue.

(Forward to Step 10, page 181)
!

SPOT YOUR CONFLICT STYLE
COMBINATION

When you chose your current partner, you were already fully armed for conflict. And so was he or she.

You also chose your partner as a fitting opponent. In the first 'in love' period, as you discovered each other, you unconsciously registered and judged each other's ways of handling disagreement. Some possibilities will have ruled a potential partner out from the very start: perhaps you personally couldn't live with someone who, under pressure, swears, sulk or walks out.

But some conflict styles mean a partner seems very attractive. It may be that you and your partner handle conflict in the same way, so you feel comfortable with familiarity. It may be that you handle conflict differently and find that the interface works: you feel flattered, reassured, in control. 'I knew I loved her when she stuck with it when I cried . . . I knew he loved me when he was so jealous he hit me . . . I knew I was important to him when he was so furious he walked out.' You really have to love someone to feel good when you push their buttons. And sometimes the way they push your buttons is proof to you that the love is mutual.

The relationship progresses. The differences between you and your partner grow, the disagreements spread, and the conflict starts to bite. And increasingly, the way your conflict styles combine becomes important. Is your combination one that will, ultimately, be positive? Or is it one that will make your relationship self-destruct?

When your styles match

Sometimes, your conflict styles are parallel. When you shout, he shouts. When you sulk, she sulks. Either both of you use one style most of the time and so they match or, more likely, you have similar repertoires and occasionally they synchronise. Ask yourself which of these matching styles you recognise, and ask yourself what you can learn from that recognition.

'We tiptoe through the tulips'
When two of you appease together, you simply don't fight. Maybe you've only just met so there are no disagreements. Or maybe – for fear of each other, lack of self-confidence, or an issue just too hot to handle – you don't want to air your resentments. This approach can work one-off, to lower the aggression level and allow you both to feel safe enough to talk. But if you carry on appeasing, then the buried anger and unmet needs leak out: in depression, sexual problems, or sneaky revenge attacks such as washing your red T-shirt with his white underwear.

'We argue over the slightest thing'
This is when both of you pre-emptively strike; you leap to the defence together. It's typical to go through a phase of this as you settle into your new relationship or, in an older relationship, ride out a temporary hiccup such as a job change or house move. Once you feel secure, you stop striking pre-emptively, and learn to sort out your differences without starting a quarrel at the least excuse. But if you don't, then emotional exhaustion can set in and you may part simply because you're so unhappy together.

'We wake the whole neighbourhood!'
High-level attack usually happens when both of you are on the edge. Something very serious is brewing, and sound and fury is

the only way you can communicate. After you've each said your piece, the attack dies away. Alternatively, you're both naturals in high-level attack, who find conflict itself is a bond you can't do without. You receive payoffs that are worth all the pain, and in the name of love, intimacy or excitement, take each other to hell and back.

'We don't really argue'

Low-level attack is the one that many couples don't use only as a style but as a way of life. They avoid head-to-head conflict, but instead engage in a debilitating war of attrition. Because you're committed to each other, it's far too dangerous to bring resentments out into the open. So you nag, blame, sulk or subtly complain. Once in a while, one of you will resent the fact that issues are never aired and explode in a high-level attack, but then settle back into solving problems by sniping. Once commitments like children are complete, you may part – to replay the whole story again with new partners.

'We avoid each other for days'

When both of you retreat together, it's probably because there's been some serious trouble. A traumatic event – perhaps an affair or a bereavement – has left you both licking your wounds, unable to express how you feel. Eventually you make contact again, recovering the bond between you gratefully. But if not, and you keep retreating, then the relationship may fossilise, leaving you unable to be emotionally intimate. Or, one of you finds a new partner whose talent is for breaking through the defence wall you set up when you retreat. You make a new start, though often this only lasts until bad feeling has built up in the new relationship sufficiently to make you want to retreat again.

'We sort it out face to face'

Everyone has some win-win styles in their repertoire, or no love relationships would ever survive. When you both use this style at the same time, things seem easy. Neither of you feels threatened by the other, so you don't need to pull out the heavy artillery. Everything goes peacefully. You both talk about your own needs, listen to each other's, agree something must be done and agree to do it. Problem over. You may not even notice there's been a conflict.

When your styles mismatch

Often, your conflict styles are different from your partner's. You shout, he sulks. You sulk, he shouts. Whatever one of you does, the other shifts to do something slightly different.

Why? One reason is the following basic, if unhelpful, rule of conflict: if what you're doing doesn't get you what you want, then settle for grabbing attention. If the going is tough, and you seem to be losing ground, then you'll often simply do something that upstages your partner, or pushes his or her buttons in some way. This doesn't necessarily mean acting like a drama queen. If your partner is already doing that, then it may be much more effective to become sullenly indifferent. The important thing is to create an effect. And more often than not, that means striking out in a different direction to your partner.

There are thousands of variations when conflict styles mix. The six below are 'classics', ones that most couples do from time to time. Which of them sound familiar to you? What do you learn from recognising them?

'You be nasty and I'll be nice'

If one of you only ever tries to keep the peace and the other only ever stirs up trouble, then one of you is using appeasement while the other is doing almost anything else. The one who is appeasing, terrified of being threatening in any way and so being rejected, becomes an expert in being kind, forgiving and loving. But, emotional dynamics being what they are, the other partner is left to be all things negative: angry, frustrated or sulking. It's almost as if there is only room for one person in the relationship to express fear and the other to express anger. Underneath, in fact, you both feel fear and anger, but in a neat division of labour, you carve up the job between you, one specialising in one of those emotions, the other in the other.

'Whatever you do, I'll overreact'

If one of you always responds with a massive and immediate overreaction to whatever the other does, then she (or he) is using a pre-emptive strike. Terrified of being forced to give in, she's upping the ante at any sign of trouble. There's nothing much that her opposite number can do in this situation, because whatever he tries, even if it's kindly motivated, she jumps in first with a counter-attack, which can lead to much hidden, hopeless resentment. In the end, he may simply lose any hope of improving things, and walk out.

'You behave badly and I'll withdraw'

If, whatever one of you is doing, the other shuts down or withdraws, then you have a combination of styles where the only stable element is that one person retreats. He (or she) feels threatened and over-stimulated by all the emotion flying about, and so cuts off in order to keep things under control. His partner may try anything she can to make contact – insults, tears, recriminations or even violence – but he just withdraws further, either emotionally or literally. The pair can end up chasing each other round the room.

'I'll act fine, then suddenly bite your hand'

If one of you suddenly and unexpectedly turns on the other, what you probably have is appeasement turned to attack. This partner has tried to keep things nice, but the effort is just too much. Instead of expressing her (or his) needs, she's pushed them down again and tried to be reasonable. Suddenly, though, it's all too much; the anger and resentment bubble up and she's snapped into attack mode. This may not happen at the time; it may be hours, days or weeks later that the post-dated recriminations bubble through. Her partner is then outraged: why has the worm turned with no warning?

'I'll be nasty, until you are too'

If one of you tries to wind the other up, but then backs off as soon as the other feels hurt, what you probably have is attack masking appeasement. The partner who's attacking has no idea how hurtful he (or she) is; he keeps attacking and attacking, until he pushes his partner over the edge. Only then does he realise with horror what he has done, and then offers anything and everything so as not to be rejected. His partner meanwhile is much too busy lashing out to respond – or may even have got to the point where she has been so hurt that she can't see peace offers as genuine, but regards them as further, disguised, attacks.

'I'll talk you down from your tree – but once you're safe, I'm off'

If one of you keeps calm during a fight, but then as soon as the good feeling starts to come back, seems to cut off completely, then one of you is using appeasement turned to retreat. She (or he) genuinely wants to make everything OK, to please her partner, to resolve the conflict. To do that, she often puts up with upsetting behaviour, and seems not to mind. But once the pressure is off, the problem seems solved and the danger over, she can cope no more and needs a complete break. Her partner, ready for a reuniting hug, may interpret this behaviour as punishment rather than self-protection, and feel betrayed.

! ———————— *Task 3.3* ————————

Mutual styles

Go back through the descriptions of mutual conflict styles. Tick or underline anything mentioned which you know you and your partner do. Are you and your partner largely using one style or a mixture?

Think of what you'd most like to change about the conflict combination you and your partner use when you argue.

(Forward to Step 10, page 181)

!

Starting to change

The main aim of this step has been to make you aware: aware of what your individual conflict styles are, aware of how you and your partner together combine styles. And this awareness in itself will start to shift your conflict patterns.

But you may also need to change your style more consciously. So here are some starting points for making that change. These are broad 'destinations': as if when you were setting off on a journey, someone told you the address you were going to, but not the roads you needed to take. As you learn more about conflict management, you'll learn more specific road directions, particular skills to halt problem interactions in their tracks. Here, though, are the general destinations to start you on your way.

- When you use an appeasement style, you're afraid that if you make trouble you'll suffer. The end result, though, is often that you simply don't have your needs met. And sooner or later, you're likely to turn round and attack your partner because you're not satisfied; or attack yourself by becoming depressed or even ill. So a much better way is to have the self-confidence to acknowledge your needs, then communicate them. In the short term, of course, this may cause eruptions. For example, if you appease much of the time, your partner will be used to your being compliant, agreeing, always saying yes. So you may receive some fairly strong reactions when you start to express your needs. Stick with it. Make sure you're not attacking or unfairly demanding. Make sure that you consider your partner's needs. But do be clear about what you want, and things will slowly start to improve.

- When you use a pre-emptive strike style, you lash out at the first sign of trouble. In doing that, you're laying down real problems for yourself. If you regularly spring to the defence before the attack even starts, then sooner or later your partner will have to do the same in order not to be overwhelmed. The alternative is to back off a bit. Wait until you have real proof of trouble. Then try to resolve things calmly rather than attacking. This may seem scary. But if you try it, then one of two things will happen. Either your partner will walk all over you, in which case you can go back to what you've been doing up to now. Or, your pulling back from the attack will encourage your partner to do the same. It has to be worth the risk.

- If you often use high-level attack, then you may think that you're a lost cause. In fact, though high-level attack is noisy and hurtful, in some ways it's easier to turn around than other styles. At least when you're shouting you're aware of your emotions and your needs. At least when you're screaming, you have lots of energy for your relationship. All you need to do is to shift the focus of that awareness and energy. Keep on being aware of what you want. Keep on going for it. Keep on trying to resolve the issues; but replace your high-level attack with a win-win style. Put your energy into creating good feeling between you, into helping your partner to respond positively, into finding a solution to problems that suits you both.

- If you often use a low-level attack style, then changing that may be particularly hard. This way of resolving issues is often unnoticeable. You pressure and harass your partner, but you often do it in subtle ways: nagging, sulking, mocking. And because everything is so low-key, you may find it difficult to admit that what you're doing is destructive. You may truly believe that it is the only way to get your needs met. The problem is that by meeting your needs in the way you're doing, you may well end up pushing your partner away by a slow drip-feed of bad feeling. It would be better to gain what you want not by hidden pressure, but by loving negotiation.

- If retreating is part of your conflict style, then your challenge is to be brave. The temptation for you is to think everything's fine; because if you don't, it feels so uncomfortable. But you need to keep in touch even when things are tough. You need to become more aware of what's happening between you and your partner. You need to gather information by keeping your eyes and ears open. You need to interact with your partner and keep interacting until you sort out what's happening between you. If you can resolve the issues, then over time you'll find the bad feeling reducing, so that in the end there will be nothing you need to retreat from.

- The ultimate aim, of course, is for you to use the 'win-win' style throughout your relationship. When you use this style, you're aware of your own needs and believe you have a right to meet them. You respect your partner's needs. You stay calm, and calm your partner down too. You negotiate until both of you have what you want. Through these strategies, you can manage conflict, and manage the differences that create it.

    The good news is that you already have the basics of the win-win style in your repertoire. They are part of being human, and socialising with others, so you're not working from a cold start. The plan is to build on the basics you already have: perhaps a deep respect for your partner, a commitment to his or her happiness, or a skill in communicating your feelings; to learn the full set of skills for win-win conflict management, and to then bring those skills into your relationship.

WHERE ARE YOU NOW?

Step 3 has helped you to learn about a number of conflict styles and where they come from, and to begin to identify your own.

As you complete the tasks in this step, remember to turn to Step 10 on page 181 and fill in the relevant sections there.

Move on to Step 4 when:

- you've understood that your way of arguing is one you learned, and that you can unlearn it and learn a better way if you want to.

- you've identified the conflict styles you use, and the ones you and your partner use together.

- you've begun to gain a sense of some of the ways in which you need to change what you do, in order to change the way you argue.

Step 4

MAKE YOUR EMOTIONS WORK FOR YOU

'We married quickly, on a high, and our very first quarrel was our honeymoon quarrel. Since then it's been hell and heaven in equal quantities. We are both very strong personalities, both used to having our own way. And we're bad with anything but perfection. If anything goes wrong between us, we'll become very emotional. We do shout, we do scream. We've never hit each other, but Debbie slammed a door in my face once, and I knocked a knife rack off the draining board and nearly sliced her foot in two. I worry sometimes, but we're calming down. It's been very difficult for both of us to adapt to the sort of give and take that partnership means. But we're getting there.' Nick

Emotions are the driving force of conflict. You fight because you feel bad. You argue because you're unhappy. You conflict with your partner because you feel strong, painful emotions: dissatisfaction, disillusionment, anger, fear.

And you want to resolve the conflict because you want to feel better. You want to feel better by meeting your needs, by being valued, by feeling that it's possible to have what you want. All of these are logical, sensible, justifiable human motivations.

It's emotion, then, that motivates you to fight. But the way to stop fighting isn't simply to halt all emotion or stop all feeling. That would about as useful as driving with your eyes shut because you're occasionally dazzled by oncoming headlights.

What you have to do is to make your emotions work for you. You have to first understand them, then to use them. They can show you where there's a problem. They can give you the energy to sort that problem. They can help you fully communicate that problem to your partner. Actually, emotions are the key to turning your conflicts around.

WHAT ARE EMOTIONS?

Emotions are life's smoke alarms. Biologically, they have their root in our body's way of showing us that something is important and needs action. Early human beings, when faced with a flood or marauding animal – or with good food to eat or a warm fire to huddle by – experienced a strong physical reaction which led them to do the right thing and survive.

Emotions are life's smoke alarms.

This physical reaction can be a shock to the system. Hormones such as adrenaline flood the body to stimulate action. Natural opiates kick in to dull any pain. Breathing rate shoots up. Heart rate jumps as many as thirty beats a minute in the space of a single heartbeat. The liver floods your bloodstream with sugar to release more energy. Blood pressure increases. Circulation speeds up. Muscles tense.

It may not be comfortable. When such body responses are drawing attention to good things – things that can make you excited or happy – then the sensations can be wonderful. But when they're signalling something dangerous, then this physical reaction is intended to be so strong and uncomfortable that it impels people to face a threat or avoid it, to take action or retreat, to choose 'fight' or 'flight'. And in the case of physical threat it still has just that effect. If you're walking past a building site and suddenly look up to see a plank falling, you move. And after you've moved, as you catch your breath and listen to your heart pounding, you thank heaven that your body has reacted so effectively.

People also feel that same sort of physical reaction when something is threatening the safety of their relationship. And they feel it when something is not literally threatening but mentally threatening. They feel it particularly when their needs aren't being met. So if you feel threatened because your partner shouts, sulks or threatens to walk out, or because you simply think: 'She's not going to agree to my holiday plans . . .' 'He's not going to have sex with me . . .' 'We're going to fight again . . .', your body will respond in the same sort way as it would if you saw a plank falling towards you. You feel a rush of adrenaline, a burst in your heart rate, a tensing of muscles. Only this time, you interpret what you are feeling not as a simple physical response. You call it an 'emotion'.

The most important emotions in relationship conflict are the same as in physical survival. They are fear and anger, the ones that lead to 'flight' or 'fight'. You imagine your partner saying 'I'm leaving' and you feel anxious and fearful. You hear your partner grumbling 'You never do what I want in bed' and you feel irritated or angry. Part of you may want to run away, part of you may want to hit back. Flight or fight.

This is fine when smoke-alarm responses are what's needed. If your partner is going to hit you, it's appropriate to run or defend yourself. But most times, fighting or flighting isn't useful at all in relationships. What's needed is to calm things down, solve the problem, sort things out, make things better.

When it comes to conflict, emotions are like small children. They're easily scared, they want instant action – and they have absolutely no sense of timing! Because of that, emotions, though as wonderful as children are, need careful handling.

Emotions, like children . . .

- . . . get easily spooked. Even if something isn't truly threatening, like a simple misunderstanding, emotions can imagine a full-scale battle and respond accordingly.

- . . . have no sense of timing. Because they're designed for instant reaction, emotions sometimes kick in long before you know what's happening.

- . . . can overwhelm you. Because they flood your body with sensation, emotions may make you less able to think clearly and respond appropriately.

- ... mix up past and present. Because their job is to alert you to what's important, if a current situation is even vaguely similar to one that has hurt you before, emotions may still react, creating an 'emotional time bomb'.

- ... confuse reality and fantasy. Triggered by thoughts as well as events, emotions can react strongly even when you only imagine a problem.

- ... may make you overreact. Because emotions work on the principle 'better safe than sorry', they can sometimes lead you to do things that are just too big for the situation.

But also, wonderfully, emotions . . .

- ... make you instantly alert. They tell you immediately something is going wrong or, in the case of more positive emotions such as excitement or joy, that something has gone right.

- ... can never be ignored. The harder you work to push your emotions down, the more they increase the signal until you have to take notice.

- ... are energetic and active. They give you the physical resources to cope with conflict, to keep going until things get better.

GEARING UP FOR AN ARGUMENT

When you and your partner come into conflict, your emotions click into gear. Some event – or some thought, or even some memory – triggers first of all a flash of fear. You may feel this flash as anxiety, as wariness, even as confusion. You typically feel it so quickly that you hardly notice it. But it's there, alerting you to the fact that something's not quite right; some need of yours isn't being met.

Here are some examples. Notice how some of these fears are based on what's actually happening, while others are much more the product of inner thoughts than of outside events.

Your partner does . . .	You think . . .	You feel . . .
He slams his fist on the table	'He's going to lash out'	Scared of being hurt
She says, 'I don't know how you can live in this mess'	'She's criticising me'	Scared of failing
He looks at another woman in the street	'He's going to have an affair'	Scared of being rejected
She sits at the breakfast table not speaking	'The last time she was in a mood like this, we had a bad fight'	Scared of yet more conflict
He says, 'Shall we go and see that film?'	'He knows I hate Bond movies'	Scared of being controlled
She says, 'I can't put up with this any longer'	'She's going to leave'	Scared of being alone
He switches on the television	'He's bored with me'	Scared of having a failed relationship
She brings home a romantic video	'We don't cuddle like that any more'	Scared of life without affection

What happens next depends very much on what you're comfortable with. It particularly links back to what you learned to do as a child when things were tough. There are three main possibilities.

Being overwhelmed by fear

'Yes, you're right . . . of course we'll do it like that . . . I'm so sorry.' You may, for example, back off. Your needs are being denied, but you let it go. You hit a disagreement, but you give in. You may even find yourself repeatedly apologising, in case something you've done has upset your partner. Your fear takes over, and you do whatever will keep you safest, and that's probably to let your partner have his or her own way, to be nice at the price of your own needs, maybe even to cry a little because you're feeling so nervous.

If you think back to Step 3, you'll realise that what you're doing is using an 'appeasement' style. Appeasement is what you do when you're stuck at the first stage of fear, when that fear leads you into the 'flight' option. It's more typical of women in Western society, because girls are brought up to appease more than boys are.

Erupting with anger

'You must ... I'm so fed up with you ... I can't believe you said that ... no way ... how dare you ...'

Fear may not lead to flight. It may almost immediately transform itself to anger, to 'fight'. This is what happens for most of us: we prefer to act and gain what we want rather than to flee and give it up. And so almost immediately that we feel afraid, we also feel angry. Most times, in fact, we don't even register the fear behind the anger, but simply the anger itself. And then we lash out: with looks, with words, sometimes even with blows.

All the conflict styles that involve attacking – pre-emptive strike, low-level attack, high-level attack – are what you do when fear turns to anger and erupts. The only difference between them is whether you tend to attack before anyone else, attack subtly, or attack at full blast. If you're a woman, traditionally brought up not to feel or show anger, you may tend to use the safer, low-level attack styles such as nagging, whinging, sulking, or being contemptuous. If you're a man, brought up to be active, you may tend to go for the high-level styles such as shouting or throwing a temper tantrum.

Disengaging from all emotion

'I'm fine, just fine ... I'm not talking to you when you're in that state ... the only thing that's wrong is that you're emotional.'

Your third emotional option is to disengage. If your fear doesn't persuade you to give in, or doesn't turn to anger and lead you to lash out, then this is what you do. It is self-protection carried to the ultimate. You find the feelings – fear or anger, or whatever – just so uncomfortable that you simply opt out of feeling them. You ignore your emotions, push them down so completely that you never feel them at all, or walk out on whatever or whoever is making you feel uncomfortable.

This is 'retreating', and men in particular do it. Physiologically, men experience emotions more strongly than women do, so feel more uncomfortable when fear or anger kick in. This is why in over 85 per cent of couples where one partner cuts off from any conflict, it's the man who does the disengaging.

The problem with all these behaviours is that, in the main, they're simply not helpful. They don't reduce the threat. They don't gain you what you want. They certainly don't improve your relationship.

Of course, appeasing your partner will keep the peace. But if in doing that you don't have your own needs met, then at some point you'll break through the terror barrier. You'll erupt into even worse anger, all ready to fuel the next battle. Or, you may simply stay stuck with your fear, which in time will transform into hopelessness, depression, or even physical illness.

There are times when anger may safely erupt. A short sharp scream can often release tension in a useful way. But though it may be tempting in the long term, erupting with anger doesn't work. It puts your partner on the defensive, and by hurting him or her, makes retaliation more likely. And if your partner does retaliate, your emotions flare up again and lead you to strike back in turn. No chance of a peaceful settlement.

There are other times when it's best to disengage. If you're on the point of physical or verbal violence, then it's best to leave the room until you calm down. Or if you're so uncomfortable that you can't think clearly, a few minutes' private thinking time will help enormously. But long term, disengagement is relationship murder. It not only leaves your partner in the lurch. It also means that the conflict is never fully resolved. You disengage because the feelings become too much for you, but if you want your love to survive, it's much better to learn how to handle the feelings.

In particular, all these unhelpful ways of handling emotion can have a deeply unhappy effect on your sex life. Your feelings, on red alert, aim to protect you from any harm that may come to you in your intimate relationship. And as the most powerfully affecting arena in your relationship, your sex life is the first line of defence. Perhaps you defend yourself by becoming unable to have sex any more: you become impotent. Perhaps you revenge yourself by becoming unable to have pleasure any more: you stop having orgasms. Perhaps you quite simply withdraw: stop feeling any desire for your partner. You do all these things unconsciously, as your emotions' attempt to protect you. But the results fuel the fire, and make things even worse between you and your partner.

Given this doomsday scenario, it may seem as if your feelings are just making trouble for you. The thing to remember, though, is that all these unhelpful responses aren't the fault of your emotions. All that your emotions do is alert you to a threat, tell you of a need or impel you to action. They don't tell you what action to take. That's your choice. If the choice is misguided, then the fault is not theirs.

If there is a fault, it's in your childhood and upbringing. Being brought up to be a sociable human being all too often means that you aren't allowed to express your emotions in the completely unrestrained way that you did when you were a few months old. And quite right too. It wouldn't be a wonderful world if people yelled with fury or hit out in anger whenever they were in the least thwarted. But unfortunately, socialisation also often means that you're taught to ignore your emotions, or encouraged to push them down so much that when you do express them, they burst out in an unrestrained way.

It's easy to make emotions the culprit in all this. It's easy to think that they're to blame when arguments develop and fights occur. But your emotions are the same whether you deal with them well or badly, whether you use a win-win style to sort out your relationship problems, or whether you appease, attack or retreat.

In fact, emotions are vital for their instant response, their activity and their persistence. You need the instinct of your emotions to tell you when something is wrong in your relationship or when your needs aren't being met. You need the energy of your emotions to start you thinking, talking, negotiating and resolving issues. You need the stamina of your emotions to keep you going until your relationship is back on track again.

!———————— *Task 4.1* ————————

Arguing variations

Think about the unhelpful ways of handling emotion: being over-whelmed by fear; erupting with anger; disengaging. Which of them do you use?

What affects your use of these ways of handling emotion? Does whether and how you use them vary according to:

● the amount of emotion: for example, you erupt with anger when you're slightly irritated, but disengage completely when things get just too much?

● what you're arguing about: you erupt with anger when it's to do with the children, but back off completely through fear if you have money troubles?

● what your partner does: you disengage if your partner starts shouting, and get overwhelmed with fear if he or she talks about leaving?

Start noticing just what affects the way you respond. Then use what you've noticed to help you spot in advance just when you need to start handling your emotions more helpfully, using the suggestions made in the next section of this step.

(Forward to Step 10, page 182)

———————— THE FIRST VITAL MOVE ————————

Whatever your unhelpful ways of handling emotion, you can replace them by more helpful ones. You can make your emotions work for you, both in the short term – in the middle of a specific argument – and long term – in your relationship more generally. The first and most important move is simply to be aware of them.

For emotions alert you to something important in your relationship. So when it comes to relationship conflict, emotions can tell you when your needs aren't being met and trouble is brewing, or when your needs are being met and a resolution is near. Emotional awareness means you have an instant and unignorable compass to guide you towards a good result.

The signals emotions send to you are non-verbal ones. They're the result of all the frantic physiological activity that prepares you for flight or fight. So if the threat seems major – your partner is shouting at you, for example – you may feel the full set of speeding heart rate, shift in breathing and rush of energy as adrenaline hits. If things are less threatening – you're simply feeling annoyed with each other – then all you may be aware of is a slight muscle tension, or a need to take the occasional deep breath.

You will also have a more individual emotional signalling system. It's often based around the 'mid-line', that imaginary line down your body marked by the spine. Organs and muscles around your mid-line are the ones that are affected first and most by the first physiological 'alert'. Stomach, chest, neck, upper back: one or more of these will be your particularly responsive area. Sudden tension between your shoulder blades, a churning in your stomach or a tightness around your chest may tell you that an argument is brewing, or building, or taking a turn for the worse. Conversely, relaxation in your upper back, a calming feeling in your stomach or a sudden easiness in your chest may be the signal that things are moving to a resolution.

When you spot these signals in your body, acknowledge them. If you simply carry on doing what you're doing, your emotions will think you haven't registered their signals, and will often increase the sensations so that you respond. Mentally clocking that you're feeling emotional – and in effect giving a silent vote of thanks for the message – is a good first move.

FIVE TIPS FOR EMOTIONAL DRAINAGE

'In the middle of our first argument, she went very quiet. Then after a moment she looked up and said "OK" and carried on, much calmer. When I asked her later what she was doing, she said, "Counting backwards from fifty". She'd learned that from her dad when she was seven. I use it at work sometimes to keep my temper.'
Michel

Once you're aware of unhappy emotions, you next need to regulate the sensations they're creating. The aim is not, repeat not, to stop feeling emotions altogether. You need emotional feedback in order to make the right next move. What you don't need, though, is over-strong physical stimulation confusing you, or pushing you to behave badly. The aim is to reach a point where you can think clearly, make decisions sensibly, and start acting in a way that will gain both of you more of what you need. Try these techniques:

- *Deep breathing:* By relaxing you, taking a deep breath sends a signal to your body that the threat isn't as huge as it seems. Your heartbeat will slow, your blood pressure drop, your adrenaline level start to dip; and you'll feel better.

- *Time out:* Another way to give your nervous system a chance to return to normal is to take twenty minutes away from the conflict situation. But to avoid simply pushing the real issues under the carpet, you need to make sure you then come back and re-engage with your partner. (For more detail on this 'time out' technique, see page 134.)

- *Distraction:* By switching your attention for just for a moment from your internal sensations on to what's happening around you, you relieve tension and make yourself more able to concentrate on what action to take. So briefly, check the number of pictures in the room, or say a nursery rhyme to yourself.

- *Positive thinking:* Your emotions are triggered by your thoughts; usually your worst fears. You can begin to calm your emotions if you briefly allow yourself to think exactly the opposite of what you fear: for example, if you started to feel scared that your partner is taking you for granted, allow yourself to remember times when he cares for you.

- *Expressing emotions safely:* Sometimes, you're so affected by your feelings that you need to let them out directly and explosively. But do this safely. So punch a pillow (not a person). Go and sit in your car, turn up the radio and scream, which is an instant tension-reducer. Write a letter to your partner expressing all the truly awful things you'd like to do to him or her, then tear the letter up. When you've got the aggression out of your system, then go back and resolve the issue.

THE EMOTIONAL CHALLENGE

When you've lowered the sensation level, then you can begin to think about what you're actually feeling. You can begin to understand just what your emotions are trying to tell you.

One good way to do this is to ask yourself three Emotion Challenge Questions: what? why? when?

- What am I feeling?
- When in the past have I felt a similar emotion?
- Why might what I fear be untrue?

These help you focus your mind on the reasons behind your emotions, and work out just what to do next in order to resolve the conflict.

Keith and Lorna have been going out for eight months, and live 120 miles away from each other. The arrangement is that they take turns visiting. But during yesterday's phone call, Keith announced that he wouldn't be able to visit on the next weekend, because a friend was having a birthday party. Could Lorna visit him instead? Lorna found herself feeling quite angry as she put the phone down.

What am I feeling?

Gather information. Find out just what you're angry about and under that, what the fear is. In particular, because emotions are usually alerting you to needs that aren't being met, you may want to explore what it is you need, specifically or generally.

Lorna's first thought was that Keith was going back on an arrangement they had made, and that seemed unfair. But delving deeper, she realised that under her anger were a number of fears: that Keith was taking her for granted, that perhaps he didn't care for her. She needed him to come to see her on the weekend they'd agreed. Her deepest need was to feel more valued by Keith.

When in the past have I felt a similar emotion?

Looking at when you've felt similar emotions in the past will help you start to work out where the feelings are coming from. If they're actually 'emotional time bombs' (past events that create overreaction in the present) then you need to realise that, and not blame your partner for the fact that you're feeling so bad. If you can gently challenge how relevant your emotions are here and now, then you'll find it a great deal easier to feel positively.

Lorna remembered two events when her emotions seemed similar. The first was that a few years ago she'd been out with a man who had let her down badly several times by not turning up for dates. She also remembered her best friend at primary school having less and less time for her when the two of them moved to different secondary schools. She realised that these memories, of being let down by people she thought a great deal of, were creating a great deal of her unhappy emotion towards Keith. She was scared that history was repeating itself.

Why might what I fear actually be untrue?

Emotional messages are useful, but they also become confused. So again challenge them. Has anything happened, recently or in the past, that would suggest that your analysis of things isn't actually true? Has your partner done or said anything positive that contradicts the negative impressions that are making you feel bad? Making a conscious effort to think clearly can bring things into perspective.

When Lorna thought clearly, she realised that Keith had offered to 'swap weekends' and come to her next time. He'd also, that week, sent her a big bunch of roses and an 'I love you and miss you' card. She thought that this suggested that Keith did still care, that she was valued. She began to feel better about everything now she realised that she had been distorting what was happening. She decided to agree to Keith's suggestion that she visit him next time. When she rang to tell him, of course, he was delighted – and that made Lorna even more confident about him and about their relationship.

Lorna could have let her anger erupt when Keith originally mentioned the birthday party. She could have let her bad feeling fester. She could have given in and agreed to visit Keith, but resented it – and been unkind to him when they met. In fact, she made it much more likely that their relationship would go well, in the short term and the long term, by challenging her emotions and making an informed decision about what to do.

It's not always easy to use these Emotion Challenge Questions when you're actually feeling upset or angry. So at first, you'll do better to practise them after conflicts, when you're not in the firing line and have time to analyse things in hindsight. In time, though, try using them on the spot, as soon as you're aware of an emotion that signals conflict; if necessary, asking your partner for 'time to think'. If you use them consistently, these ways of challenging your emotions can prevent painful conflict because you'll find yourself calming your feelings down before you even have a chance to behave unhelpfully.

CRUNCH POINT: CAN YOU TAKE RESPONSIBILITY?

'I felt resentful for months because he'd never seemed keen on what I was doing. It was only when I overheard him boasting to his mum about me that I realised that the bad feelings were mine. He was proud, but I'd wanted enthusiastic jumping up and down, and, of course, Josh simply doesn't do that reaction about anything at all.'

Dana

Of all the stages in learning to handle your feelings, this next one is perhaps the most challenging. In order to make your emotions work for you, you have to take responsibility for them.

It's a very real temptation to do just the opposite. It can seem so attractive to blame your partner: 'You made me feel angry . . . When you were late, I felt so frightened.' There seems a clear link between your partner's behaviour and your emotions, a clear cause and effect between these things and what you feel. So it's very logical to turn on your partner, in your head and in reality, then blame him or her for all your bad feeling.

It's tempting, but of course, it isn't useful. And more often than not, it isn't accurate. It isn't useful to blame because doing that doesn't make your partner change and be more the way you want. All it does is raise the bad feeling between you and make it more likely that you'll behave badly to each other in the future.

And, blaming all too often isn't accurate. For as we've seen your emotions may be leading you astray. They may be confused, mixing up past and present, flooding in with no sense of timing to over-alert you to a danger that has very little to do with your partner and everything to do with you.

So try to acknowledge that while your partner's behaviour may be a trigger, your painful feelings may be because of an event that happened to you years before. Consider the possibility that your painful emotion is leading you to make muddled interpretations. And be prepared to accept that you could have a part in what's happening: that what is happening might be due, for instance, to the fact that you can't accept the differences between you, that you're unwilling to settle disagreements, that you aren't fully clear about what you need.

If you can start to take this kind of responsibility for your feelings, you'll immediately find it twice as easy to cope effectively with what is happening. You'll think more clearly, respond more appropriately, act more rationally. And, ironically, you'll then be much more able to resolve the issue and gain more of what you want.

SCREAMING AND SHARING

The next step in making your feelings work for you is to share them. For human beings have an instinctive need to communicate their emotions. When they do, often the pain goes away and what is left is relief and energy, energy that can be used to take action.

Have you ever seen a child fall over? As she (or he) starts to wail, she immediately looks round for a grown-up to wail to. And once that grown-up is there, listening to what's happened, the little one is able quite quickly to forget the pain, dry the tears, and carry on playing. In just the same way, sharing your feelings will help you to feel better and more able to cope with the situation.

Sharing your concerns will also help your partner to understand, be more able to empathise, feel better about you. And it will also give you both a chance to realise that you have a need, a problem, and then to act as a partnership to meet the need and solve the problem.

There is a 'but'. Fear creates hearing loss. If what you say or do

---

Fear creates hearing loss.

as a result of your feelings means your partner feels frightened or angry too, that will lead to an unwillingness and an inability to even hear, let alone respond to, what you are saying.

That doesn't mean to say there's no place for the short sharp scream. If you open the freezer door to find that the 2-litre tub of chocolate-chip ice-cream you bought yesterday evening has mysteriously 'disappeared', then a loud yell may well be irresistible. And it certainly isn't forbidden. Conflict management doesn't mean you never ever raise your voice. It's particularly apt if you're letting off steam; if you know that a short, sharp scream will reduce the tension and let you communicate much better with your next sentence. It's also particularly apt if a short sharp scream gives you, as a couple, the chance to communicate emotions and needs that you simply wouldn't otherwise express, or to release energy that you can then use to resolve the issue.

But the scream should be short and sharp, not extended and brutal. Communicating strong feeling needs to be the single, one-off starting point of a process of resolving the issue. It shouldn't be a whingey, blamey battle that lasts for hours or days and never achieves anything. It needs to be a genuine expression of what your needs are, before you then go on to meet those needs in more subtle ways. So by all means have a scream. But keep it brief and then move on.

As you move on, what's the best way to share your emotion? First, some practical dos and don'ts. Don't start in when you or your partner are upset, stressed or have been drinking; do choose a time when your are rested, clear headed and able to concentrate. Don't share private emotions in public or in company; do find a place clear of distractions where you won't be disturbed. And don't just leap in; set a framework and make it positive: 'I know we've had a problem with this, and I want to find a solution that will suit us both . . .'

Let's look at an example of what happens when emotions aren't well expressed, and so things go badly wrong.

Elaine and Neil come home from work. Elaine's had a good day, and is looking forward to a relaxing evening. Neil's furious. Elaine forgot to fill up the car with petrol, so he ran out on the way to work. He comes into the kitchen as Elaine's taking the fish out of the fridge for supper.

What happens	What's happening underneath
Neil says angrily: 'Elaine, how many times must I tell you, if you use the car, don't leave the tank empty.'	He tells her off, bullies her, blames her.
Elaine says defensively, 'Oh, Lord. Did I use that much? Was it a problem?'	She'd meant to stop off at the garage. She feels guilty and upset because he's so angry.
Neil says angrily 'A problem? Yes, it ran out this morning. I was only half an hour late for work. That didn't go down too well, did it? But that's just like you. You always forget. You never remember anything. Even your mum complains about your lack of memory. You know how I hate it, but still you always do it. Why do you think the car's got a petrol gauge?'	He attacks her verbally.
Elaine says in an irritated way, 'Look! I'm just as busy as you are. How come I'm expected to remember everything? You don't!'	She's started to feel that all this is unfair.
Neil shouts, 'Everything! I'm talking about one simple thing! You make me so angry!'	Again, he blames her for his emotions.
Elaine slams the fridge door as she runs upstairs.	
Neil slams the house door as he goes out for the evening.	

Where does Neil go wrong? From a standing start of pent-up emotion he puts Elaine on her guard by his body language and aggressive voice, then attacks. Particularly, he uses sweeping accusations, which leave Elaine resentful. It's not at all helpful to generalise about all the awful things your partner 'always does', or to bring in other people's resentments as fuel for your battle.

And, Neil blames Elaine completely for his own emotion: 'You make me so angry.' He makes no attempt to explore or to take responsibility for his own feelings, no attempt to appreciate Elaine's point of view.

Of course, Elaine's response wasn't perfect either. Both partners drove the situation in an unhelpful direction. But things would have gone better if, at each point, Neil had done something more like this . . .

What happens	What's happening underneath
Neil says calmly 'Elaine, can we talk? When I used the car this morning, the tank was empty.'	He introduces the subject gently and tries to smooth the anger from his voice.
Elaine says guiltily, 'Oh, Lord. Did I use that much? Was it a problem?'	She'd meant to stop at the garage, and feels bad about that, but is largely reassured by Neil's voice tone.
Neil says calmly, ' 'Fraid so. I ran out on the way to work. So I was late. I do actually feel quite angry about it. I know you didn't mean to forget. But I've been thinking about it, and I realise that when you leave me with an empty tank, when you just forget, I feel I'm not important.'	He explains the problem, explains how he feels, and takes responsibility for his own feelings.
Elaine says comfortingly, 'Of course you're important to me.'	She didn't want him to break down on the way to work, and responds to his feelings.
Neil says supportively, 'Can you find a way to remember? I could remind you if I know you're going to use the car. Or perhaps you could put a post-it note on the dashboard to remind you. It'd be great if you could do that.'	He suggests action.
Elaine says happily, 'Fine. No problem.'	She'll be likely to want to follow Neil's suggestions.

Here, Neil introduces the subject gently. He's careful not to attack Elaine. He tells her clearly what his feelings are so that she can start to sympathise and see his point of view. He speaks about his own experience directly, genuinely and keeps to the point. He shows that he has realised that his emotions are his responsibility. He also suggests action; tells Elaine what he'd like to happen. He paints a picture of what his needs are and appeals to her to help him meet those needs.

To tell your partner how you feel is to invite him or her into the most intimate part of your life. So it's vital not only to share your emotions in a way that your partner can empathise with, but also to communicate that your emotions are yours. That's why it's particularly important not to use blaming phrases such as: 'You made me . . . When you do this, I have to . . .' Instead, try saying simply 'I feel . . .'

Here are some ways that work when sharing emotion:

- Use non-threatening body language, particularly voice tones.
- Use 'I feel . . .'.
- Don't blame your partner for your emotions but take responsibility yourself.
- Avoid sweeping accusations or unfair complaints.
- Explain how positive your emotions would be would be if your needs were met.

IS ANY ACTION THE RIGHT ACTION?

The emotions you feel only have one aim in life. They want you to take action. They want you to act to meet your needs: surface needs such as making sure you still have some chocolate-chip ice-cream, or deeper needs such as being looked after or respected. The bad news is that if you don't take action, your emotions may well stir you up until you do. The good news is that emotions not only help you take action by giving you energy, but tell you 'well done' by shifting their signals from uncomfortable to comfortable when you've succeeded in taking action.

So what sort of action should you take? A good deal of the time, simply sharing your emotion is enough. The fact that your partner understands what you're saying and gives you sympathy may actually meet whatever need you have for respect, for understanding, for love. But often, something more needs to be done. You may want practical activity, as Neil did when he suggested he remind Elaine to fill the car up. You may want an agreement or a promise, as he did when he asked her to use post-it notes on her dashboard. The action may be much more wide-ranging: you may want to make a further commitment, divide responsibility more evenly, decide to have a baby, or aim to add more interest to your love-making.

All these issues require more than just resolution. They require discussion. They require negotiation. And they may require large amounts of both over long periods of time. In order to hold that discussion or create that negotiation, you need further skills; and these are covered in detail in Steps 7 and 8. When you've gained those skills, use the energy and the motivation that your emotions give you to put them into practice.

!━━━━━━━━━ *Task 4.2* ━━━━━━━━━

Practising the six steps

Read back over the six steps to handling emotions helpfully: becoming aware of your feelings, draining your emotions, challenging your emotions, taking responsibility, sharing your emotions and taking appropriate action.

Next time you find yourself feeling emotional when with your partner, take a moment to practise the first step, emotional awareness. How does that awareness affect you? Does it have any effect on your partner?

Each step in handling your emotions follows on from the previous one. It's difficult to do those later in the sequence if you haven't mastered those earlier on.

So once you feel that you have practised emotional awareness, move on to practising emotional drainage . . . then challenge . . . then taking responsibility . . . then sharing your emotions . . . then taking action. Don't expect immediate results. But do notice – and give yourself a round of applause – when what you are doing starts to make a difference.

(Forward to Step 10, page 182) **!**

EMOTIONAL TIME BOMBS REVISITED

'Up until two years ago, if I felt trouble brewing, I'd immediately go into what Jimmie called my "shrew" act. I'd become very shrill and sarcastic, and emotionally push him away. Then Sophie was ill, and we had to decide whether to let her have an operation or not. He said yes, I said no, but I couldn't push him away that time because we had to keep talking and make a decision. I felt this wave of anger and tears. I kept thinking that I couldn't trust him to make the right decision. But that was so unfair; he'd always been there for me. After Sophie came home, I was talking it through with an old friend. She said, almost immediately, "But you've never had a trustworthy partner". And she was right: neither of my two previous husbands ever coped. My first was just weak, the second was a gambler. Of course I never trusted Jimmie, because I never knew men could be trusted. I started seeing a counsellor, and that helped a lot. Now, if we have a problem, I don't push Jimmie away. I trust him enough to talk about it.'

Sara

You can do so much by coping with your emotions in the here and now. You can use the techniques mentioned in this section to acknowledge, challenge, share and act on your feelings as you feel them. But sometimes, an emotion is especially huge. It triggers such strong reactions that none of these techniques work.

Often, as we've seen, the emotion you feel when you're in conflict with your partner has nothing to do with what's happening in the present. Instead, it's about an 'emotional time bomb', a past event where you felt betrayed, maybe in your relationship, often outside it, typically from your childhood.

Time bombs are particularly likely to result from deep trauma such as violence, abuse or abandonment. But they may not have been created by a traumatic incident. If you ever felt even slightly insecure, disliked, punished or unloved – particularly when you were very young and vulnerable – this may have felt to you like a betrayal. And now, in a situation even remotely like the past one, you react as if you're again being betrayed, and the normal tools for managing emotions simply can't cope.

If you find that you sometimes have difficulty in handling your feelings, you may have a time bomb lurking. This is particularly likely to be true in arguments where what you're feeling seems out of all proportion to what's happening; where what you're feeling seems unlinked to what is happening; where you hit out physically or verbally or are often afraid you'll do so.

If these things ring a bell for you, find a listening ear. Sharing emotions is always a good idea, but particularly so in the case of emotional time bombs. So ask a friend or your partner to help you talk things through.

● Take as your starting point the feeling that you seem to be unable to cope with, or the incident that triggered it. Do either remind you of an earlier event; of someone other than your partner who hurt you; of a particular time in your life?

● If you contact a strong memory, which seems somehow similar in emotion to the feelings you struggled with, remember more about what happened. Tell the person listening all you can about the incident you remember. Give details of what you saw and heard, and what was done and said.

● Particularly, allow yourself to feel the emotion you felt in the past. You may not have been able to do that at the time, so take the opportunity now to express the fear, the grief or the anger. It may help to 'replay' the event a number of times, to allow yourself more than one chance to express all your emotions.

● Finally, remind yourself that, however painful that event was, it was in the past. Today, you're a different person, much wiser, stronger and able to cope with what life brings. You don't need to be hurt now as you were hurt then.

Be careful. Don't confide in a friend or partner if what you're talking about is too close to home. For example, it's not fair to expect a pregnant friend to sit still while you talk about the time you had a miscarriage, or expect your spouse to stay calm while you talk about the time you had a passionate affair. (Particularly if a partnership issue has become a 'no-go' area which you simply can't talk about without fighting, you need to handle the whole thing in a different way. Step 5 offers suggestions.)

Also, don't use this method if what you suffered was very traumatic. It's fine to rely on those close to you to handle memories that leave you crying or angry: being let down on a 'date', or having your pet rabbit die. But it's unwise to ask them to cope with memories that leave you hysterical or overwhelmed with rage: abuse or rape, for example.

In both situations – where an event is close to home, or where it's traumatic – you'll find it very useful to talk to a counsellor. They can offer the support and sympathy that a friend or loving partner would offer, but with none of the disadvantages. They'll always put you, rather than themselves, at the centre of the conversation. They'll always keep secret everything you tell them. They'll let you say what you want, and express whatever emotion you want, without judging you. They won't be shocked or embarrassed, whatever you say and whatever you reveal. They won't push you into revealing, or talking about, things you don't want to. And they'll keep supporting you until the past emotions are no longer having a bad effect on your present relationship. For all these reasons, you may want to defuse your emotional time bombs with the help of a professional. If you do, then About Relate (page 188) gives some suggestions about what to do.

! ================= *Task 4.3* =================

Defusing the time bombs

NB: This is a task to do only if you feel that there are emotional time bombs in your relationship.

If an emotional time bomb is causing problems think through your options. Could you talk to your partner and resolve it that way? Could you talk to a friend you can trust? Could you ring a help line? Could you go for counselling?

(Forward to Step 10, page 182) !

Whoever you talk to, once you've explored what happened in the past, what you typically find that the hurt gradually disappears. Once expressed, past resentment often just fades. You can literally feel the pain begin to fall away. You can start to feel confident that, whatever the argument, it will not be built on a foundation of overwhelming fury. You can start to hope that in future, conflict will be something you can handle. Once again, you start to look your partner in the eye and see someone you love.

WHERE ARE YOU NOW?

Step 4 has helped you to understand how emotions kick-start your arguments, and to start expressing your emotions in the most useful way.

As you complete the tasks in this step, remember to turn to Step 10 on page 182 and fill in the relevant sections there.

Move on to Step 5 when:

- you've started to understand that emotions are useful, that you can make them work for you, but that there are helpful and unhelpful ways of acting on them.

- you've identified how you personally use your emotions.

- you've started to practise ways of using emotions more helpfully within your relationship.

RE-UNDERSTAND YOUR PARTNER

'We laugh about it now. But at the very worst times, during that month, I would actually fall asleep hating her. It seemed so unfair that she wouldn't move in with me, that her family was more important than I was. I kept thinking that if she loved me enough, she would do it. Of course she was right to wait. If she'd have walked out then, with her father dying and her mum not coping, she would never have forgiven herself – and probably have never forgiven me. She was scared of losing me, but she knew that I'd wait. She was far more scared of losing her mum and dad's love if she just upped and left. But I didn't realise that. I just kept on trying to reason with her, convince her, argue her into it.'   Darren

Be honest. Whether or not you've admitted it yet to anyone but yourself, you do feel critical of your partner. You may not feel bad about everything he or she does, just over one or two big issues that seem to catch a raw nerve. Or over several irritations, that trip you up whenever things seem to be going well. Or, over a host of tiny pinpricks, but ones that increasingly take the shine off being together. Whatever, the differences between you are now chafing, and criticism is now part of your relationship.

If you want to stop arguing, you have to stop criticising. However much you realise what you're doing in an argument and why, and however much you make your feelings work for you, you can't move forward if your partner is still someone whose behaviour confuses and so irritates you, whose approach to life rubs you up the wrong way; in short, someone who seems almost like an aggravating alien.

There was a point earlier in your relationship when your partner wasn't alien, when you sympathised and empathised. In short, there was a point where you understood. What you have to do now is to '*re*-understand'. You have to rediscover your partner's identity, feelings, thoughts and motivations all over again. If you can do that, you'll stop criticising. And if you can do that, you'll be well on the way to stopping the arguments.

THE DISILLUSIONMENT PATH

But how did you reach this point? What brought you to the stage where you're so critical? Meet the Disillusionment Path, a set of clearly defined phases through which a relationship moves if it's not handled properly.

At first, of course, everything is rosy. You meet, you fall in love, you make love. You enjoy giving to each other, and feel that you receive in return. You tend to use the 'win-win' style of interacting, because you're feeling so good and so unthreatened that it never occurs to you to go on the defence or on the attack. In any case, you feel so in tune that you're sure you'll never think or feel differently from each other, and that you'll never disagree.

It's a myth. Every person is an individual and therefore different. And in time, these differences start to show. Maybe you welcome them, as refreshing or complementary. And if you're one of the remarkable couples who can always celebrate each other's differences, then your relationship will flourish. You'll do what works: build on your complementarity to meet each other's needs. So where one is lacking, the other gives strength. Where one has tunnel vision, the other supplies a wider viewpoint.

For many couples, though, the story develops along different lines. One of you says something that the other can't agree with. One of you asks something, and the other just can't oblige. If you're practised in using win-win styles of conflict management, then at this point you use all your skills to resolve your disagreements: expressing your feelings, communicating your needs, negotiating to gain a resolution. If you succeed, the relationship flourishes.

If you don't or can't succeed, then conflict builds. You each try to persuade the other to agree or oblige. You begin to appease, to attack, to retreat. That feels awful, so you kiss and make up. But the problems begin again, and this time they're worse. You are on the Disillusionment Path.

The Disillusionment Path

Stage 1:	Falling in love	Aware of similarity	Able to give
Stage 2:	Moving closer	Aware of difference	Willing to give (some couples stay at this stage, celebrating each other's differences)
Stage 3:	Beginning to worry	Aware of difference	Less able to give (some couples at this stage use conflict management skills to resolve the difficulties their differences cause)
Stage 4:	Trying to resolve things	Ignoring difference	Giving in hope (many couples move on to this stage and carry on down the Disillusionment Path)
Stage 5:	Building suspicion	Resenting differences	Feeling resentful about giving
Stage 6:	Being in conflict	Attacking and defending differences	Refusing to give
Stage 7:	Feeling hopeless	Hating differences	Fully disillusioned

Stage	She says	He thinks	He says	She thinks
Stage 1: Falling in love, aware of similarity, able to give	She says 'Why don't we go out for a meal?'	He thinks 'That'd be lovely, though I like staying in too.'	He says 'Of course. That would be wonderful.'	She thinks 'We're so in tune.'
Stage 2: Moving closer, aware of difference, willing to give	She says 'Why don't we go out for a meal?'	He thinks 'I'm tired, but it's lovely that she's so energetic and sociable.'	He says 'We'll go if you like, though I'd much rather stay in and relax with you.'	She thinks 'He works so hard, and it's great that he wants to be with me. Of course we'll stay in.'

Stage 3: Beginning to worry, aware of difference, less able to give	She says 'Why don't we go out for a meal?'	He thinks 'Not again!'	He says 'No, I'm too tired tonight, love. Maybe on Saturday.'	She thinks 'Where's this great social life he said he liked?'
Stage 4: Trying to resolve things, ignoring difference, giving in hope	She says 'Why don't we go out for a meal?'	He thinks 'I do want things to work.'	He says 'Of course. I don't want us to fight about it.'	She thinks 'I'm worried we're starting to argue.'
Stage 5: Building suspicion, resenting differences, feeling resentful about giving	She says 'Why don't we go out for a meal?'	He thinks 'Nag, nag, nag.'	He says 'You know I'm exhausted. Why don't you think on?'	She thinks 'He's always exhausted. Never a thought for me.'
Stage 6: Being in conflict, attacking and defending differences, refusing to give	She says 'Why don't we go out for a meal?'	He thinks 'I'm sure she does it deliberately. She knows I work hard and need a break.'	He says 'Give it a rest! If you can't stop going on at me, I'm going to bed.'	She thinks 'He just goes out to hurt, every time. He knows how desperate I feel if he just cuts off like that.'
Stage 7: Feeling hopeless, hating differences, fully disillusioned	She says 'Why don't we go out for a meal?'	He thinks 'I can't stand it. She's never going to get off my back.'	He says 'I'm going out.'	She thinks 'Why do I bother? It'll never change. We're doomed.'

As a relationship develops, there may well be some horrifying shifts. In the end, you may start to believe that your partner is acting the way he (or she) does because he wants to hurt. And of course, if each of you believes that the other is acting with malicious intent, then that alters everything. You start to believe that your partner isn't someone you can love, or trust, in any way. You start to fear that things will never change. You start to think that you have to protect yourself – by defending or attacking – just in order to survive. You start to believe the relationship will never be a happy one. And whether you stay together or part, then if you continue down the Disillusionment Path, you'll never recover the good feeling of the early days.

!================= *Task 5.1* =================

Good news differences

Differences are at the heart of relationship problems. But often, it's differences that brought you together in the first place.

On a piece of paper draw two vertical lines so that you create three columns on the page.

In the left-hand column, make a note of five ways in which your partner is different from you, differences which originally attracted you in the first place. Perhaps he was more easy-going than you are ... perhaps she was more ambitious.

In the middle column, opposite each of the five differences, write down whether this difference now causes arguments, and if so how. Perhaps his easy-going ways mean nothing is ever done. Perhaps the fact she's ambitious means she never talks about anything but her job.

Now the challenge: in the right-hand column, write down how – in spite of any problems – each difference between you and your partner has made the relationship better. His easy-going nature may mean that he's never stressed. Her ambition may mean you're never short of money

Differences can be a problem. But they can also be an opportunity.

(Forward to Step 10, page 182) **!**

_____ IS THERE A WAY HOME?_____

Is it possible to go back along the Disillusionment Path? Is it possible to retrace your steps emotionally back through the stages, to the point where you and your partner are sufficiently in tune with each other that you can resolve your differences and celebrate them?

It is possible, but it needs deliberate action. To do this, you have to re-understand your partner. You have to begin to see why your partner is as she (or he) is, and why he (or she) is different. You have to see that these differences are natural. You have to see that what your partner does, even if it irritates you, isn't viciously motivated.

And, much harder, you have to reach a point where you understand that your partner's attacks and defences aren't viciously motivated, either. You have to begin to understand just why your partner lashes out at you or shrinks back from you.

All this isn't easy. If arguments are a regular part of your relationship, then even if you're only a few yards down the Disillusionment Path, you'll find it difficult to even want to re-understand. You may be afraid that if you even let down your defences a little, your partner will behave even more badly towards you, will want control, will take over: in short, that you'll end up running your whole life the way your partner tells you to.

It's unlikely. All the evidence shows that if you try to understand your partner, then in time – even if she (or he) doesn't put equal effort into comprehending you – there will be a shift. Your partner will relax and stop attacking. She will let down her defences. She will begin to feel able to give you more of what you want.

THE EVIDENCE COLLECTOR

Your first move must be to re-understand what's on the surface; what your partner says and does. For a few yards down the Disillusionment Path, you reach the point where you view his (or her) behaviour, and tend to interpret it pessimistically. You tend to think it means something negative, when in fact the intention was just the opposite.

Let's take an example. Rachel walks into the kitchen, where her partner Derek is having breakfast. He looks up and says the words: 'The milk's off.' But what does Rachel actually hear? Depending on the situation, her mood, and the stage she's at along the Disillusionment Path, she may hear a simple piece of information: 'The milk's off.' She may hear an implied criticism: 'The milk's off and you should have noticed it.' She may hear high-level frustration: 'The milk's off, it's always off, and I'm sick and tired of its being off.' Or, if she is in the final stages of the Disillusionment Path, she may hear a deliberate intention to hurt: 'The milk's off, and I'm blaming you because I want to make you suffer for what you did to me yesterday.'

The first interpretation will probably cause Rachel no problem. The other three, more pessimistic interpretations, are likely to leave her unhappy, defensive and liable to attack. And if she's already far down the Disillusionment Path, those are the ones she is most likely to hear, the interpretations she is most likely to make.

In fact, she'll probably be wrong. To be precise, she will probably have heard something that's at least two or three levels of aggression higher than was meant. But Rachel won't realise that. To her, Derek's comments will be proof positive that things are badly wrong in their relationship.

How can you find out if you're interpreting your partner incorrectly? How can you understand exactly what your partner does and says? How can you, particularly, begin to re-understand what your partner really means?

The following Behaviour Evidence Collectors will help you work out what's going on when your partner seems to be behaving unhelpfully. The six Collectors are: look, listen, check, remember, remember more, investigate.

Use them in the same way as you used the Emotion Challenge Questions from Step 4. Some of them are parallel questions, but this time applied to your partner's behaviour rather than to your emotions. Begin by using them at the earliest opportunity after any worrying interaction with your partner. They'll help you reflect and understand what happened. As you gain more practice, use the Behaviour Evidence Collectors as you interact with your partner, to analyse anything he does that seems threatening.

- *Look at your partner:*
  Ask yourself . . . is there any evidence from my partner's body language that suggests that my pessimistic interpretation isn't true?
  Rachel could gather, from the apologetic smile on Derek's face, that what he's really saying is that it's the milk he himself bought yesterday evening which is off.

- *Listen to your partner:*
  Ask yourself . . . is there any evidence from what else is being said that suggests that my pessimistic interpretation isn't true?
  Rachel's partner's next words might be: 'Let's be wicked and go out for breakfast?'

- *Check your mood:*
  Ask yourself . . . when I'm feeling differently, would I interpret this differently, more optimistically?
  Rachel might realise that she has a hangover, and has just had a bill through the post, and so she might be particularly prone to interpreting things pessimistically.

- *Remember:*
  Ask yourself . . . is there any counter-evidence from what's been said or done recently that my pessimistic interpretation isn't true?
  Rachel might realise that Derek looks so annoyed because the milkman has delivered rancid milk for the last three days.

- *Remember more:*
  Ask yourself . . . when this has happened before, have subsequent events proved my pessimistic interpretation right or wrong?
  Rachel might realise that Derek is always in a bad mood in the morning, and always cheers up after a large bowl of cornflakes.

- *Check out:*
  Ask your partner . . . a question that will gather further evidence, such as 'How are you feeling this morning?'
  Derek might look surprised and say: 'Absolutely fine. Isn't it a great morning, love?'

This final suggestion – to check out what's actually happening – isn't only one of the most useful things to do. It's also the most "uncomfortable". It's the most useful course of action because often it will show you that your partner's words and actions are harmless: he's not out to hurt, he's motivated by something other than maliciousness. So checking what was really meant can, in the short term, defuse a nasty situation by reassuring you about your partner. Long term, too, checking out in this way is useful because it will teach you to be more optimistic about your partner and his actions. It can start you walking back along the Disillusionment Path to the point where you believe the best of each other.

But checking with each other what you're feeling may be uncomfortable. It means admitting that you thought the other person was 'behaving badly'. And if you don't handle this carefully, your partner can feel criticised and go on the defensive. So try not to start in attack mode, accusingly or presupposing problems: 'I know just what you're thinking . . . You're upset, aren't you? . . . I can tell you feel annoyed.' Instead, ask supportively: 'How are you feeling? What are you thinking? Are you doing OK?' If you show that you're not jumping to conclusions, your partner will be far less likely to leap to his own defence.

SO WHY THE BAD BEHAVIOUR?

You've checked out just what your partner thinks and feels, either mentally, or by asking. In many cases, you'll discover that your worst fears were unjustified: your partner was not out to attack you. But sometimes your worst fears do come true. Derek may have responded to Rachel with some curt and critical sentences about how useless she is in the kitchen. Your partner may have admitted that she (or he) acted as she did because she feels bad – about you.

If so, don't panic. What you need to do is carry on re-understanding. You need to look behind what's happening on the surface – criticism, wariness, sharp voice tones – and find out what's happening underneath. You need to carry on re-understanding not only your partner's behaviour, but the reasons behind her behaviour.

Think back to the previous section of this book, Step 4. Think back to your analysis of why you yourself so often lash out at your partner, withdraw, defend, or attack. Your 'bad behaviour' may not be the same as your partner's. But if you want to understand your partner's reasons for behaving badly, start by thinking about your reasons for doing the same. Remember that if your needs aren't being met, you feel strong, painful emotion that tells you something is wrong. So does your partner. You're impelled by these emotions to flight or fight. So is your partner. These emotions of yours are often illogical, often confused, and often given to overreaction. So are your partner's emotions.

The main emotions you feel are anger and fear. Those are your partner's main emotions. And whichever emotion you show, the underlying one is fear. As it is for your partner. Whichever emotions you feel, expressing them unhelpfully is all too tempting. It's tempting too for your partner. And it is very easy to justify unhelpful reactions because you feel so threatened. Your partner, unsurprisingly, feels the same.

The truth is that your partner is exactly like you. Confused, hurt, needy, defensive, and above all afraid; what you feel is what your partner feels. The reasons why your partner behaves badly are identical to the reasons why you defend or attack. And your partner's key feeling, the one that underpins everything else, is exactly the same. Fear. If at any point, at any time, in any way, your partner seems angry with you, it is because of fear.

Here are some examples of the many things that your partner may be afraid of:

being rejected	being unloved
being abandoned	being attacked from behind
being accused unfairly	not being respected
being criticised	being taken over
being destroyed	not succeeding
being a total failure	being abused
being attacked	being made fun of
being invalidated	being trapped
being hurt physically	not being fulfilled
being hurt emotionally	being overwhelmed by emotion
living unhappily	dying unfulfilled

Your partner's fears come from two original sources. The first is you, and your behaviour. When you lash out, it's easier for your partner to feel frightened she's going to be hurt. When you turn away, it's easier for your partner to feel frightened he's going to be abandoned. And in this sense, yes, you are involved in the fear your partner feels.

Here are some ways that you may be doing this. You may well be able to think for yourself of many more.

When you do or say . . .	Your partner may think . . .	Your partner may well fear . . .
Back down or give in (appeasement style): 'Yes of course . . . whatever you say . . . of course I don't mind.'	'I know she doesn't mean it . . . I'll get it in the neck later.'	Being accused or attacked unfairly.
Go on the offensive, lash out first (pre-emptive strike style): 'Before we start, I don't want to hear any more about . . . I know what you're feeling.'	'What's coming next?'	Being attacked from behind.
Shout, scream, throw, hit (high-level attack style): 'How dare you, how can you . . . I hate you.'	'She must hate me . . . I'm scared of her . . .'	Being seriously threatened, hurt, abandoned, emotionally destroyed.
Accuse, be sarcastic, blame, correct, complain, contradict, criticise, demand, interrupt, judge, mock, nag, show contempt, sulk, think the worst, whinge (low-level attack style): 'You're so stupid . . . I suppose you think I'll fall for that one. Why can't you do a simple thing like . . .'	'As far as she's concerned I'm unlovable . . . a failure . . . a joke . . .'	Being unloved . . . not being respected . . . being a failure . . . being made fun of . . . being trapped . . .
Deny your emotion, emotionally withdraw, turn away from, leave (retreat style): 'I'm fine . . . I just don't want to hear it . . . I can't stand it when you're so emotional . . .'	'She's going to walk away . . . I'm never going to be secure.'	Being abandoned, rejected.

The way your partner feels when you do these things is a powerful argument for making sure that you do them as little as possible. But even if you personally never triggered any bad feeling in your partner, this still doesn't mean that she would never feel bad, or act badly. For the second source of your partner's bad feeling, the one that's responsible for the deep and compelling emotions, is nothing to do with you and everything to do with the past. The vast majority of the fear that your partner feels will be from way back in life, when she was far more vulnerable than she is now.

'Dad brought me up on his own and he made sure I knuckled under over everything. Ben lived in an area where there was a lot of rough stuff going on. We were fine until Thomas was born, then suddenly everything went wrong. I wanted more help in the house, Ben was working full time. We were at each other hammer and tongs. I couldn't work out why he was suddenly behaving so aggressively and he felt the same about me. We worked it out in the end. At the start we'd both felt safe with each other. But then suddenly I was faced with this big man telling me what to do, just like my dad. And he listened to me shouting and kept remembering being beaten up.'
Alison

Remember how you earlier learned about past painful experiences and how they create emotional time bombs in your mind? Your partner too has time bombs, buried memories of past betrayals that come to the surface during conflict. Alison's experiences with her father made her particularly vulnerable to Ben's aggression. Ben's memories of being beaten up meant that he felt threatened when Alison nagged him.

Of course, your painful interactions with your partner trigger the fear. But it also triggers fearful time bombs for which you're not directly responsible. So your partner's defensiveness or aggression isn't only at you. It's also at the parents who told her off, at her brother who hit her . . . at the schoolmates who wouldn't be friends with her unless she acted cool . . . at the teacher who wouldn't listen when she tried to explain . . . at her very first sexual partner who left her . . . at her first husband who wanted his own way over everything. All the people in your partner's life with whom she couldn't resolve conflict in the past are here with you when you're arguing in the present.

When you can fully take all this on board, a big breakthrough can happen. When you truly realise that your partner's actions are based on fear as well as on anger, then it can radically change the way you feel about her. When you truly realise that much of her fear and anger really comes from the past rather than the present, then it can radically change the way you behave towards her. Rather than shouting your partner down, you may well feel more like listening. Rather than hitting out, you may well feel more like offering a cuddle. And rather than being disillusioned, you may well feel more like retracing your steps and beginning to love again.

! ═══════════════ *Task 5.2* ═══════════════

Digging for fears

From what you know of your partner, which of the fears listed above seem to you to be most likely the ones that he or she feels?

Where in the past, perhaps, did your partner's fears come from? You probably know enough about his or her childhood, early life and early relationships to make an informed guess.

If you're able to swap notes with your partner about this, then tell each other your fears.

(Forward to Step 10, page 182) !

SIX WAYS TO DISARM YOUR PARTNER

As you feel better about your partner, you'll be able to act better towards him (or her). This will help a great deal. For if you alter the way you act, that will create a difference to the way your partner reacts. If you can show him that you understand him, and he feels understood, then he will begin to stop attacking you, and begin to let down his barriers.

It may take a while. Your partner not only has to start believing that he no longer needs to be afraid of you. He also needs to wipe away a lifetime of being afraid of anyone with whom he's been in conflict and who has hurt him. You may have to show your understanding many times, over days weeks or mon ths, before your partner can fully believe in it. But when he does, it will change things.

You may be having your doubts about all this. If so, take a moment to imagine a scene. Imagine that you're sitting opposite your partner. Through words and body language, you know beyond a shadow of a doubt that he or she is trying to understand you, and is slowly becoming more and more able to understand your feelings, why you act as you do, what you want from the relationship and why you want it. If your partner really did understand you like this, how would you feel? About your partner? About your relationship? About yourself?

The real point of this 'exercise in imagination' is, of course, that it works both ways. If your partner really tried to understand you, you would immediately feel more positive towards him or her. If you really try to understand your partner – and can show that you do – then your partner will want to start reciprocating.

So here's how to show your partner that you understand him. It will be particularly important to use these suggestions when he is expressing strong emotions or deep needs. And this will often be in the heat of an argument when feelings are high. But if you can use these skills at other times – when your partner confides in you, when he has a problem – then you'll find that the understanding they communicate to your partner will also work to improve your relationship.

1 Show your partner you empathise

The body language that most shows understanding is also the body language of attention and sympathy. Turn towards your partner, look at him, offer a touch if that seems appropriate. Using this body language not only signals understanding to your partner; it also has an effect on your concentration, actually making you more able to take in and comprehend his words, even if at first you're feeling critical.

Then, as your partner talks, let your body language adapt to show that you're feeling with him. So if he smiles, and you want to smile, then do so. If he is sad, and you feel yourself taking on a sad expression, then let that happen. Couples who deeply understand each other often sit, stand and move in total synchrony, so although forcing yourself to do this won't help, allowing yourself to naturally follow your partner's movements will signal your empathy.

2 Acknowledge your partner's emotions

You won't be surprised to realise that, more than anything, your partner needs his emotions understood and accepted. So bring feelings out into the open and acknowledge them, not in any kind of critical or mocking way, but by using questions such as 'How do you feel about that?' and encouraging phrases such as: 'I understand you're angry . . .' 'This must be difficult for you . . .' 'Thank you for telling me that . . .'

Particularly, resist the temptation to rush in with a solution to any problem your partner may have before you've fully understood the emotions involved. Men in particular often feel that if a difficulty arises, it's their role to fix it as quickly as possible. In reality, as mentioned in Step 4, both genders need to share their feelings fully before they're ready to take action. So hold back from suggestions – 'What we ought to do is . . .', – and concentrate on questions: 'What are you worried will happen if we . . . ?'

3 Appreciate your partner's viewpoints

You can understand your partner and still not agree with his viewpoint. But you do need to appreciate it. So while you don't need to go along with what your partner says, thinks or feels, it is important to show that you value his perspective. However tempting it may be to put your partner right, argue a case, or give your point of view, it will pay much bigger dividends if instead, you allow him to express his view and then show your appreciation of it. 'I understand that . . . yes, I see how you can think that.' Particularly beware 'tit for tatting': where your partner expresses an emotion, or a dissatisfaction, and you counter it with a more painful one of your own, leaving him feeling belittled: 'You hated clearing up after the party? You should see what I do every day!'

4 Recognise your partner's needs

Hand in hand with your partner's emotions and viewpoints are his needs. These may be practical: he needs help with papering the bathroom. They may be psychological: he wants support in coping with the kids. They may be surface needs: he wants a cuddle. They may be more subtle needs: he wants to know you love him. If you can show your partner that you grasp what he needs, then he will, quite simply, feel better. Try saying: 'What you seem to need . . . you're telling me that what you want . . .' Or on a deeper level: 'I understand that you don't feel valued . . . in control . . . successful. I understand you want things to be different.'

5 Be prepared to act

The ultimate sign of understanding is willingness to take action. If you share someone's perspective, then you want to act on that perspective. Again, this doesn't mean agreeing to do exactly and only what your partner wants: you have equal rights here. It does mean being willing to put time and energy into resolving the issue, whether that be your habit of eating toast in bed, or your partner's habit of needing more or less sex than you do. This willingness, just as much as words and smiles, is your partner's guarantee that you really do understand.

6 Show your love

However you feel about your partner's behaviour, showing that you care is the best way to show real understanding. You'll have ways of showing your love that are particular to your relationship: a tight secure hug, a sympathetic tone of voice, a wide and happy smile. These things are what originally led your partner to fall in love with you. Done genuinely and with feeling, these are your strongest allies in reducing your partner's wariness and showing him that there is no need to be afraid. The minute you feel a little sympathy, a little affection, a little love no matter how small, then show it clearly in the way you know best. It will make a difference.

! ================ *Task 5.3* ================

Panic buttons

Make a list of things that you know you do that push your partner's panic buttons: walking out, being sullen, raising your voice. How do you imagine your partner feels when you do these things?

If you can, ask your partner specifically what he or she needs to calm down: a smile, a touch, a particular reassurance? If you can't check with your partner, use your knowledge of him or her to make your list. How do you imagine your partner will feel when you do these things?

(Forward to Step 10, page 182**)**

These ways of behaving are the basic building blocks for turning your conflict styles around. But of course they're not necessarily straightforward to achieve. For your partner may not be explaining his feelings in a way that's easy to accept. He may be expressing views that are different to yours, showing dissatisfaction with you, voicing disagreement. And he may not be expressing all this in an easy-to-accept way. He may not know, or be able to use, any of the positive ways of expressing emotions. He may be blaming you, nagging you, interrupting you, accusing you; in short, behaving unhelpfully.

If so, you'll need to make an extra effort to re-understand, particularly to recognise your partner's deepest fears. For under every angry word, there will be a fear lurking. If you can spot it, recognise it and imagine how your partner feels when he's as frightened as that, then you'll find it much easier to respond in a useful way.

A final warning. Sometimes, with some partners, understanding and showing your understanding isn't enough. This may be particularly true if your partner is addicted to drugs or alcohol, is seriously depressed, or tends to become violent. If your partner shows signs of doing any of these things, then first of all, find extra help for yourself, perhaps from your family or friends, perhaps from a specialised support group. Particularly, if your partner becomes violent, then make sure you can always leave the room (or the house) under your own steam for as long as necessary; and make sure you have a safe place to go.

After that, if at all possible, gain support for your partner. Explain that you'll support him or her to see a professional by giving time, energy, money or hand-holding. The Appendix makes some suggestions. But don't nag or pressure your partner. Expert help only actually works if it's willingly received. You can take a partner to a counsellor, but you can't make him (or her) change.

CAN YOU EVER FORGIVE BETRAYAL?

'Just after my sister committed suicide, Pam had an affair. It lasted about two months, and she only told me afterwards. We stayed together, and Liam was born a year later. But I felt deeply hurt and every time we had a serious argument, I'd drag out the affair and wave it in Pam's face. That lasted for years. Then her dad died and the roles were reversed. I don't think I'd ever realised up to then just how hard it had been for Pam when I was recovering from my sister's death. I'd been depressed, totally cut off from her, and for a while she thought she'd lose me. It was no wonder she'd turned to someone else for comfort. For the first time, I understood what had happened, and we were able to talk about it.'   Simon

Your partner may have done something particular that left you feeling betrayed. This may be a single event, like Pam's affair. Or it may be an issue that has built up resentment over time: for example, you resent the fact that your partner hates your best friend. If so, there is good news and bad news. The good news is that if you're able to re-understand your partner, you'll start to feel better about any previous betrayal.

The bad news is that you may need to deal with the betrayal specifically before you're able to start to re-understand. Particular resentments can mean it's difficult to even want to sympathise with your partner. Your emotions, badly hurt before, scream at you not to let your guard down. Phrases such as 'It'll only happen again' and 'Why should I listen after what she did?' will spring into your mind.

To move forward, you need to lay the past to rest. You can go so far in clearing up your arguments without forgiving each other, but you can't go the whole way. There are five main routes to forgiving a partner who's hurt you. Which one of them could help you begin to forgive?

- You may forgive because what your partner has done is now irrelevant, or even seems harmless. Think through what happened. Particularly if it was a long time ago, you may find that it is no longer important. If so, then forgiveness may not be an issue any more.

- You may forgive because the positive aspects of your partnership outweigh your partner's unhelpful behaviour. What does your partner give you, what does she contribute to the relationship? These things may balance out the past. If so, you may be able to forgive.

- You may forgive because your partner is genuinely sorry, and you know from this that she'll never hurt you in this way again. If so, you may not need to hold your lack of forgiveness as a defence weapon any more.

- You may forgive because you now understand and appreciate why your partner did what she did. You now see that she made the only choice she could. If so, you may be able to sympathise and let the whole thing go.

- You may forgive because you've realised that in some way you share responsibility for what happened. Perhaps your actions encouraged your partner to act as she did. Perhaps your actions made it easier for her to act that way than any other. This kind of thinking may seem a challenge: it's much more tempting to put all the responsibility on your partner than to accept some of it yourself. But with courage, you may able to acknowledge your part in things. And if so, you may feel much better about the role your partner played.

If you've not yet forgiven your partner for something, then you need to put effort into doing this, sooner rather than later. If you can forgive, then you have a chance to improve the present as well as healing the past.

! ================== *Task 5.4* ==================

I forgive you

NB: This is a task to do only if you can swap notes with your partner, and if you feel you've made real progress and are putting your problems behind you.

Is there an issue from the past that you still haven't settled between you? If so, set time aside to talk it through.

Using all the supportive strategies explained in this step, explain to each other your individual experiences of the event, your reasons for doing what you did, your emotions and particularly what you were each afraid of. Be particularly careful not to lapse into blaming.

When you reach a point where you feel you've fully understood each other, and have both been able to admit your part in what happened, then apologise and express sympathy to each other.

Then, put the past behind you.

(Forward to Step 10, page 182) !

================== TURNING 'I' TO 'WE' ==================

'When he lost his job, the first few weeks were bad. I was at my wits' end. I was used to having the place to myself once the kids were at school, but now he was under my feet the whole time, sitting in the living room filling in forms. If I came in to ask how he was doing, he'd accuse me of checking that he wasn't watching the TV. It was the career counsellor who helped. She asked us both in, started us talking about how we felt. For the first time I understood he thought he was a failure because they'd given him the push. And he'd thought I was thinking the same. I didn't; in my eyes it was the firm that was the failure for going bust. Once we were clear about that, we starting supporting each other.'

Jayne

Re-understanding your partner will make a positive change. It won't only help when you're having an argument, when your understanding will help your partner to reduce his or her negative feelings and so behave better. As mentioned earlier, re-understanding will also reverse your progress down the Disillusionment Path. As you understand more, as your partner starts to return that understanding, you'll find you feel less and less suspicious.

Crucially, you may also find you're aware of your differences but that you value them rather than resent them. For remember that it is the differences between you which potentially make you both compatible. If the two of you were absolutely the same, then you'd have the same vulnerabilities, the same gaps in your vision. When faced with problems, you'd come up with the same – and not necessarily the right – solutions.

If you can trade on your differences, to fill each other's gaps and broaden each other's vision, to support each other's vulnerability and fulfil each other's needs, to swap strengths and exchange insights, then the very differences that used to annoy may well make you ecstatic. You may actually start to think that you are stronger as two than you are as one, that you are more effective in the world together than you would be if you were on your own.

And then you may start thinking of yourselves once again as a part of a couple rather than simply as two individuals struggling to make a partnership work. You may start saying 'we' rather than 'I', 'Let's do that together' rather than 'I'm doing that on my own', 'Why don't we?' rather than 'Why should we?'. In particular, you may start to feel able to give again: to consider each other's needs, see them as just as important as you own, and then meet them.

As you start to feel your new commitment taking hold, build on it. Don't let it slip away. So spend time together. Do things together. Tell each other what has happened during the day. Start learning in detail just how you tackle life in your individual ways – and how this makes each of you the person you are. And, start showing in detail just how each of you can help the other to solve life's problems – big and small – more effectively by offering a new and fresh viewpoint.

The more you know about the differences between you, the more valuable they will seem, and the more you'll be able to appreciate them.

WHERE ARE YOU NOW?

Step 5 has helped you re-contact the feelings you once had for your partner, particularly by re-understanding him.

As you complete the tasks in this step, remember to turn to Step 10 on page 182 and fill in the relevant sections there.

Move on to Step 6 when:

- you've recognised that you have to re-understand your partner if you're going to rebuild your relationship.

- particularly, you've started to appreciate that your partner's unhelpful behaviour is really based on a single emotion: fear.

- you've started to develop ways of helping your partner reduce that fear and realise that you do understand and care for him or her.

LEARN TO DRIVE THE ARGUMENT PROCESS

'The moment I started to hope that we could make it work was one day last summer. I was at my parents', and we'd spent the day together. But then he asked if he could stay over, and of course he couldn't, and he was sulky. Every time before, I'd been irritable at him, and felt he was trying to pressure me. But as we started to become tense, and I started to feel our voices rise, I thought: "I'm not going to let this happen again." So I put my arms round him and gave him a hug, and reminded him that when we were back at college, we'd have all weekend to sleep together. I literally felt him relax. And I thought: "If I really think about it, I can make things work." And then I knew it would be all right.' Suzanne

You've come a long way. You've laid many foundations by understanding, thinking, feeling, and practising skills. Now, you're going to start working directly on the arguments themselves. You have to develop active tactics: to spot a fight as it starts, curb it, then turn it into a constructive discussion which takes the issues and sorts them out.

This may seem impossible. When it comes to unstoppable forces and immovable objects, try a runaway train, a herd of wild horses or a loving couple in the full flood of a fight. So you may laugh despairingly at the thought that anything could stop you and your partner arguing.

But it can be done. For although it may seem as if the whole thing is out of control, it isn't. In fact, either one of you can stop an argument in its tracks or more usefully, steer it gently into new tracks, those of resolution rather than confrontation.

The reason it's possible to do this is that an argument is like a dance. It takes two moving together, in synchrony if not in harmony, each affecting the other.

You feel tense, your partner acts edgy. In response, you cast your eyes up to heaven, while he slams the crockery. So you let fly with an accusation and he follows up with a whinge. In turn you appease, attack, retreat, or whatever. Each of you affects the other, and each is affected. Who started it? The question is meaningless. You each affect the other so speedily that it's impossible to tell. What started it? Who knows. Each element that followed the other was so tiny that an observer probably would never have spotted the first tiny negative thought, which speedily triggered the first negative feeling, which rapidly sparked off the first negative body language, which led to the first angry word.

But all this is good as well as bad news. The fact that you each affect the other means that either alone can turn the argument round. The fact that you affect each other so quickly means that you can make things better just as rapidly as you can make things worse.

And the fact that an argument is impelled by tiny shifts of behaviour is also good news. It means that it may only take a tiny shift of behaviour to slow the fight down and stop it. You, or your partner, or both of you together, can drive an argument towards the point where you can start to communicate and resolve the issue. It takes one angry frown to start an argument. It may only take one sympathetic smile to bring it to an end.

There's an extra bonus. If you successfully drive or steer the argument, then you not only reduce the bad feeling and prepare the way for resolution. You also hold out the promise that next time you begin to argue, you'll be able to do this again, more successfully, and earlier. Then each future time you succeed, you become more able to build on success. In the end, you may get to the point that if either of you even tilts the argument in a positive direction, you'll both act together to push it all the way there.

ANATOMY OF AN ARGUMENT

How does an argument develop? The diagram shows how. Triggers lead to your thinking and feeling unhelpfully. Perhaps an issue is raised, or a need isn't met. Sooner or later (sooner, if you tend towards pre-emptive strike tactics) you communicate that subtly in words and body language. You carry on at this subtle level for a few minutes, a few hours or, if you tend to use low-level attack styles of argument, for days, weeks and months.

You can, of course, ignore what's going on, never admit the problem, never resolve the issue, never even make up; this is particularly likely if one of you is prone to retreating. Or, you can bring it all out in the open, letting the low-level attacking build slowly until you can't ignore it, or precipitating a crisis in true high-level attack style. After which, either a kiss and make up (or a no make up) ending, with no attempt to sort out what went wrong. Or, a win-win decision to sit down and resolve the issues, which is much more likely to reach a result.

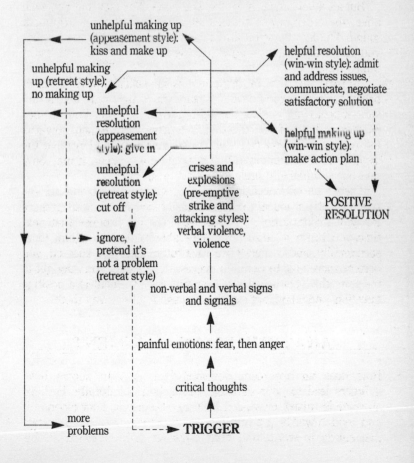

unhelpful making up (appeasement style): kiss and make up

unhelpful making up (retreat style): no making up

helpful resolution (win-win style): admit and address issues, communicate, negotiate satisfactory solution

unhelpful resolution (appeasement style): give in

helpful making up (win-win style): make action plan

unhelpful resolution (retreat style): cut off

crises and explosions (pre-emptive strike and attacking styles): verbal violence, violence

POSITIVE RESOLUTION

ignore, pretend it's not a problem (retreat style)

non-verbal and verbal signs and signals

painful emotions: fear, then anger

critical thoughts

more problems

TRIGGER

So how do you drive this process? Remember that the aim isn't just to feel good. It's to move the argument to the point where whatever has created the bad feeling is sorted: differences aired, disagreements settled, issues resolved. The aim is to drive the argument to the point where you can talk about things, negotiate about them, and move on with your relationship improved.

_____HEADING IT OFF AT THE PASS_____

'My first wife was a real problem. I'd like to use a stronger word. If I sensed we were feeling tense and said something, she'd go all moody on me. Our arguments were always over the tiniest thing, real 'squeezing the toothpaste in the middle of the tube' stuff. She'd always say there was nothing the matter and ask why I was flying off the handle. And that would often last for days. In the end it wore me down. Helen's so much better. It took me a while, when I was first with her, to even mention that I thought there was a problem. But I soon learned that if I feel we're heading into deep water, she'll respond. She'll give me a hug, or make a joke, and then we can talk about it.'   John

The first skill you need in driving an argument is being able to spot the earliest signals. You're probably aware of most of them already. Inside you, you sense trickles of barely noticeable anxiety, then trickles of far more obvious irritation. From your partner, you sense a vague tension, or a shift in voice tone. Or, one of you mentions a 'taboo' topic that you know will lead to trouble.

Here are twelve key argument predictors to watch out for.
Your inner emotional signals:

- You begin to think critically about your partner and what he or she is doing.
- You start feeling general and personalised signals of fear: for example, churning tummy, tense back.
- You start feeling general and personalised signals of anger: for example, a rush of energy, tense chest muscles.
- You decide that it's better to have an argument than to keep the peace.

Signals between you:

- You stop interacting with each other and are more silent than usual.
- You turn away from each other and don't look each other in the eye.
- Your voices change in pitch slightly as tension tightens the vocal chords.
- You check with each other: 'Are you OK? Everything all right?' and receive an irritated response.
- You start contradicting each other: 'No . . . I don't agree . . . you're wrong.'
- You start questioning each other: 'Why did you do that? Are you sure?'
- You use controlling language: 'You mustn't . . . You shouldn't . . .'
- You feel uncomfortable with, or shrink away from, touching each other.

! ================= *Task 6.1* =================

Spotting the signals

What tells you that an argument is looming? Complete these sentences:

Inner signals that I feel inside are . . .

Outer signals that I show are . . .

Outer signals that my partner shows are . . .

Topics or issues that trigger an argument are . . .

Keep your eyes and ears open for these signals in the future.

(Forward to Step 10, page 183)

!

Many of these predictors, on their own, don't seem as if they are signals of full-scale conflict. But they are signs of trouble. A tight voice tone, even if the words are friendly, signals tension. A contradictory phrase, even if the voice tone is friendly, signals disagreement. The greater the number of these argument predictors you spot, the greater the chance of a fight. If you hit a combination of any three together, then you almost certainly have trouble brewing. But even one signal means you should take action.

And one of the easiest ways of acting is actually to halt the argument as it starts. If you can divert your interaction into good feeling, then you can usually head problems off at the pass.

For this, you can use the process: Relax, Review, Reach out.

● *Relax:* one of the main things creating the problem is mutual tension, passed from one to the other of you and building slowly. This puts you both on the defensive, and therefore more likely to attack. So before you do anything, relax as much as you can. Shift in your seat; take a few deep, slow breaths. Alter your body language so that it seems more friendly. Drop your voice tone so that it sounds less threatening. You'll immediately feel better, your partner will pick that up and be less tense, and this in turn will help you to relax further.

● *Review:* next, think about what's happening and what needs doing. What are your emotions trying to tell you? This is a time when, if you can, you should use the Behaviour Evidence Collectors or the Emotion Challenge Questions to review what your partner is really doing and what you're really feeling. Perhaps the tension is just coming from stress or tiredness, and there isn't an issue to be resolved at all; you've both had a bad day and just need to wind down. Perhaps there is an issue to be resolved or a need met but now is neither the time nor the place. Or perhaps conflict is imminent and needs fixing immediately.

● *Reach out:* do what needs doing, which is almost always to make contact. In the case of stress or tiredness, this might be simply to say: 'We've both had a rotten day. Do you need a hug?' In the case of an issue that needs to be tackled, or a need that has to be met, this might be to say 'Should we talk about it now . . . this evening . . . when your mum and dad have gone home?' Make these suggestions in as positive a way as you can, without challenging or confronting, and then arrange when and where you'll both feel ready and able to discuss and negotiate.

A final point here. If it's your partner and not you who first spots the problem and uses Relax, Review, Reach Out, you have a choice. You can either block your partner's efforts to de-escalate the conflict, or you can support him or her to do so. It can be tempting to respond to an olive branch by using a flame thrower, because by the time an olive branch is necessary, you may feel more like striking out than being reasonable. But remember that you both have an equal part to play in heading things off at the pass. Do your best to respond, to calm down, to meet your partner half-way. Just because your partner is being 'good' by making a peace offer doesn't mean to say that you have to be 'bad' and turn that offer down.

It can be tempting to respond to an olive branch by using a flame thrower.

TWELVE WAYS TO DRIVE AN ARGUMENT ALONE

What if you don't notice bad feeling early? What if you can't head it off? The next possibility is that you can divert it into more positive channels.

To begin with, here are some useful techniques you can do yourself. You may find that just one technique does the trick, or that you need to use lots because the bad feeling is taking a while to fade. Don't be discouraged if things don't improve immediately you try any of these things, or if you reach a result and then minutes later a chance remark sets the argument off again. Just keep your head and keep trying.

Some of these strategies, though, just won't work in some partnerships. The trick is to try them all out a few times, keep the ones that have an effect and dump the ones that don't. Particularly, dump the ones that mean your partner feels worse. Some men, for example, hate women using humour to halt an argument because they feel laughed 'at' rather than 'with'; while a woman may react badly if a man uses heavy innuendo. (Vice versa though, can work a treat!)

Play with the timing

Painful interactions, like good comedy, stand and fall on timing. They usually speed up as they become more heated, then slow down when things are calmer. Try de-escalating an argument, particularly in its early stages, by simply slowing down your voice and movements, and leaving slightly longer gaps between the interactions.

Do something unexpected

Breaking the rhythm can lead to a completely different dance. So one way to disrupt an argument can be to simply alter what you normally do. Particularly if you and your partner have a regular argument about the same issue, or a similar kind of argument at recurring intervals, do something unexpected. If you usually shout, try smiling. If you usually smile, try admitting clearly you're unhappy. Do almost anything that will create a different response and see whether this shifts the interaction from argument into communication.

Use humour

A well-placed joke has a good chance of instantly lightening the situation. This won't work at all if the joke is cruel, sarcastic or if it's aimed at your partner. It has more chance of working if it's aimed at yourself or something outside the situation, and if you both genuinely find it funny. Stop at once if you sense your partner is feeling laughed 'at' rather than 'with'.

Use sex

Making a sexy comment can work wonderfully if you're not deep in conflict. It instantly takes your minds off what's happening and onto pleasure; a pleasure that both of you share. It's more risky to make a physical pass, but this can also be successful if skilfully done. If the pass develops into something more, it can distract you from the argument altogether, so make sure you take the time afterwards to resolve any outstanding issues.

Expose your feelings

Talking about your feelings is an excellent way to feel better, as explained in Step 4. But many counsellors report that it's also one of the most powerful techniques of all to turn an argument round. For often, knowing you're vulnerable will help your partner understand and sympathise, and so respond. But only refer to what you're feeling, take responsibility for it and never slide into blaming your partner for what you feel. Remember that 'I feel very sad . . .' is much more useful than 'You're making me cry'. Make sure, too, that you give your partner a full chance to talk about his own feelings.

Comment on the situation

It can help to imagine yourself looking at your interaction from the outside, and then to comment on what's happening: 'What's going on here? I think I'm getting defensive . . . oh yes, I always feel like this when we talk about my sister.' Drawing attention to what you're doing may well allow both of you to realise what's going on, then slide you gently into stepping outside the bad feeling and taking action.

Make sure you speak personally, and that what you're saying doesn't criticise your partner: so 'My voice is rising, isn't it . . . ?' will work where 'I always end up shouting when I'm with you . . .' won't. Particularly effective is to comment about what's happening that is positive – that you're feeling better or more relaxed, or more loving – because in making you both feel more confident of success, it increases your chances of succeeding. Be wary though: that strategy won't work if your positive comment is a vain hope of your interaction improving, rather than a genuine comment on the fact that it is!

Ask for more information

A variation on commenting is to ask for more information about what your partner is thinking, saying or feeling. This will not only allow him (or her) to feel appreciated, so less threatened and less likely to hit back. It will also start your partner thinking more deeply about what's happening, becoming aware of what his emotions are telling him. It will help him become more in touch with what's going on for him. Remember to ask gently and unchallengingly, using phrases like: 'What do you feel? . . . What are you thinking? . . What are you worried about? . . . What do you need in order to feel better? . . . Explain to me how? . . . Tell me more about why? . . .' Then listen carefully and supportively to the answer.

Jerry wants Kim to slow down a bit because she's been ill.

J: 'Why don't you take things easy over the next week or two, love?'

K: 'No way. You just don't understand. If I don't get the back bedroom painted, it won't be ready when Chris and Julie and the kids come for Easter.'

This response would move things in an unhelpful direction:

J: ' Well, that doesn't matter. You shouldn't worry about that!' Kim will feel she's in the wrong, and will go on the defensive.

This response would move things in a positive direction:

J: 'OK, tell me more about that. Explain to me why that's so important to you.' Kim will realise that Jerry's trying to understand and support her. She'll relax as she gives him more detail, and will then be more likely to listen to his point of view.

Say you're sorry

True love isn't 'never having to say you're sorry'. It's being willing to say you're sorry. A genuine apology is an incredibly effective way of interrupting a fight and turning it into a more co-operative venture. It won't work, though, if it's not genuine, or if you're only apologising because you're frightened that if you don't, there'll be more trouble. In that situation, your underlying lack of sympathy will show through, your partner will sense it and feel no better.

True love isn't 'never having to say you're sorry'. It's being willing to say you're sorry.

Clara's spent a lot of time at her brother's corner shop lately, and Laurie has had to look after the kids on his own.

L: 'I know your brother needs you to help him in the shop, but this is getting to be a real strain. The kids don't know when you're going to be here.'

This response would move things in an unhelpful direction:

C: 'Well, that's just the way it is, I'm afraid . . . It certainly isn't what I want.' Laurie will think that Clara isn't worried about the effect on him or the family. He's likely to start striking back.

This response would move things in a positive direction:

C: 'I'm sorry, love. I promised him until the end of the week, and you know I like to stand by my word. After Friday, things will be a lot better . . .' Laurie will realise that Clara regrets what's happening as much as he does. He's likely to be sympathetic.

Reward what you want more of

If you want your partner to do something, then the best approach isn't to punish the behaviour you don't like. Instead, reward the behaviour you do like. Unfortunately, it's easy to forget this. If your partner suddenly starts to do something positive, such as calm down or admit you're right, it's tempting to throw in one final insult just to make sure you have the last word, and of course this doesn't help. Instead, reward positive behaviour. You don't need to make a big thing of it. Often the most rewarding thing is the simplest: a smile, a loving touch or an enthusiastic comment.

Jason's not happy because he wants to try different positions in bed and Paula's a bit wary.

J: 'Could we just try this one, love? It looks really fun, and we don't need to carry on if you're not enjoying it.'

P, relaxing and starting to feel more confident: 'Well, OK, let's give it a go.'

This response would move things in an unhelpful direction:

J, feeling he's made his point, so rushing in to make that point even more strongly: 'Thank heaven, I thought we were stuck with the missionary position for the rest of our married life!' Paula will feel punished, and back off again.

This response would move things in a positive direction:

J, with a smile and warmth in his voice: 'Fantastic. It really means a lot to me that you're willing to try it.' Paula will feel rewarded, and be more ready to co-operate.

Tackle the fear head on

Before attempting this strategy, you may need to stop and remind yourself of what you learned in previous steps – all conflict is based on fear. All the other painful emotions, such as anger, link back to that fear. The point of remembering this is that often, rather than trying to stop the angry behaviour, you can actually defuse a fight by tackling the fear directly, either in yourself or in your partner.

If you can do that, then you do have a good chance of success. Because if either one of you stops being frightened, then you will stop needing to use the destructive behaviours that lead to an argument. And, your partner will react by becoming less fearful themselves. Then, in a neat reversal of the way you got into the argument – winding each other up into conflict – you'll start winding each other down into becoming calmer and more likely to make peace.

However, tackling the fear head on isn't the easiest of strategies to use. You need to think fast, because once fear takes hold, an argument can escalate very quickly. You need to think clearly, because it's tricky to spot fear in yourself or your partner, particularly when the bullets are flying. And you need to be flexible, because whatever you or your partner does, it often isn't clear exactly what you're afraid of. But it's certainly worth, in any fight situation, trying to stem the fear at source.

The table on the opposite page gives a few suggestions of likely fears and possible ways to defuse them. You may want to explore what you and your partner's particular fears are, and work out your own customised versions of these suggestions.

When you or your partner's response is to ...	You might be doing this through fear of ...	When you catch yourself doing that ...	When you catch your partner doing that ...
... back down or give in (appeasement style)	... losing each other's love if you make trouble in order to get what you want	... reassure yourself that with your increasing skill, you can have what you want without alienating your partner	... help your partner to realise you're not going to reject him if he doesn't give in to you. 'I don't think you're happy with that, and that's fine. I do want to meet your needs. Let's talk about what would make us both completely happy.'
... go on the defensive, lash out first (pre-emptive strike style)	... being unsafe, being caught unawares	... reassure yourself that you can cope, whatever happens	... calm your partner's fear by backing off and not attacking. 'My guess is that you think I'm trying to ... scared that I will ... worried that ... how can I help you feel more secure?'
... shout, scream, throw, hit (high-level attack style)	... being seriously threatened, hurt, abandoned, emotionally destroyed	... reassure yourself that you're not in real danger (if you are, then leave the room); take time out to calm down	... help your partner by suggesting you both take time out to calm down; a cuddle may help if your partner is hysterical
... whinge, demand, sulk, interrupt, judge, mock, nag, contradict, (low-level attack style)	... not having your needs met, of not having what you want	... reassure yourself that you're already learning more effective skills to gain what you want	... calm your partner's fear by reassuring him that he won't lose out. 'I'd like to know what your needs are. What do you want? We can negotiate on that.'
... emotionally withdraw, leave (retreat style)	... being overwhelmed by the situation	... reassure yourself that you can cope with what is happening; use the skills you know to reduce the sensations	... calm your partner's fear by quiet words or silence; withdraw for a while: 'Why don't we agree how long we'll take apart, then come back here to talk in X minutes?'

Make an offer

Listening to what your partner needs and wants, and then offering to meet that need, is a master stroke. It doesn't just bring you to the point in the argument where you can start communicating and negotiating your needs. It doesn't just help your partner feel valued and good. More than that, once it's part of your regular repertoire, it builds trust. Both of you start to feel that your needs can actually be met in your relationship, and once you start to believe that, you'll tend to be much happier, more encouraged and more motivated to meet each other's needs.

One warning. Don't expect your partner to offer something in exchange the first time you do so. It may take a while for her (or him) to recover from the shock of receiving a peace offer. It may take even longer for her to believe that it's a genuine offer, a genuine sign that things are improving. But once the penny drops, then this strategy will make a difference.

Carly wants to make love now. Terry's got an important meeting in the morning.

T: 'I want to make love. But I know you prefer it when we take our time, and I really need an early night.'

This response would move things in an unhelpful direction:

C: 'Don't be so silly. You can manage that meeting standing on your head, and anyway, having sex'll make you feel great in the morning.' Terry will think that Carly doesn't appreciate his worries, and isn't prepared to do anything about them. He's likely to get more worried still.

This response would move things in a positive direction:

C: 'Well, why don't we make this one a quickie, just for you. Maybe tomorrow night, when you're more relaxed, you can give me a return match!' Terry will realise that Carly's willing to give something to him, because she realises the problem. He's likely to feel reassured and loved.

Meet the Fundamental Need of the argument

There's a point in arguments where, for many of us, what we're arguing about gets forgotten. It's almost as if our focus narrows, and all that matters is what's happening now. We become motivated by Fundamental Needs, not in regard to the issue, but in regard to the argument itself. We want to feel valued, in control and successful – during the conflict. We may want our partner to show us respect in the argument so we feel valued; to stop pressurising us so we feel more in control; to at least see our point of view so we feel successful. We battle on in the vain hope we'll gain these things, and then won't need to battle any more.

All this provides a very useful tool with which to drive an argument. For if you can start to meet your partner's Fundamental Needs during a fight, then he or she may well feel better immediately. (Conversely, of course, if you deny a Fundamental Need, saying or doing something that leaves your partner even more scared of being unvalued, out of control or unsuccessful within the context of the argument, he or she will be more likely to respond unhelpfully.)

There is a 'but'. If you fulfil your partner's Fundamental Needs at the expense of your own, then this strategy will backfire. Your own Fundamental Needs will, short term or long term, stir up your emotions so that you feel even more uncomfortable. So if what you say leaves you yourself feeling devalued, puts you in an 'out of control' position, or puts you down, then this strategy simply won't be effective.

Owen and Victoria are in the middle of an argument about whether Victoria should ask for a pay rise at work or not.

V: 'I just don't feel able to ask for a rise yet. I've only been there four months.'

If Victoria needs to feel more valued *in this argument, this response would move things in an unhelpful direction:*

O: 'You're so weak when it comes to going for what you want. I sometimes wonder why I ever fell for you.' If Victoria feels that she isn't valued, she's likely to react badly.

This response would move things in a positive direction:

O: 'Well, I think you do well enough to be given a pay rise.' Allowing Victoria to feel valued allows her to concentrate less on fighting Owen and more on making the right decision.

If Victoria needs to feel more in control *in this argument, this response would move things in an unhelpful direction:*

O: 'But you have to. You must. How do you think I'll feel if you don't?' Pressuring means it's less likely that Victoria will want to consider Owen's views.

This response would move things in a positive direction:

O: 'I'd like you to go for it. But you have to do that when you feel ready.' Leaving Victoria to make the decision means it's more likely that she will listen to Owen's points.

If Victoria needs to feel more successful *in this argument, this response would move things in an unhelpful direction:*

O: 'You're wrong. You've been there long enough to be given a rise.' If Victoria feels she's in the wrong, she's more likely to fight on.

This response would move things in a helpful direction:

O: 'I do see what you mean. I just feel that you deserve it, however short a time you've been there.' Acknowledging what's right about what Victoria says will let her start to consider what Owen is saying.

!========== *Task 6.2* ==========

Driving lesson – Part one

Think back over the strategies you can use on your own. How easy would you find it to use when you were arguing? Rate each of them on a scale of one to ten, giving the easiest to use 10, and the most difficult 0.

Next time you find yourself arguing, use the '10' strategy first. If it works, go on to use strategy 9, and so on. Keep practising until you can use at least half of the strategies you've listed.

(Forward to Step 10, page 183)

!

SIX WAYS TO DRIVE AN ARGUMENT
TOGETHER

This next group of strategies can only be used if both of you know what's going on. You work together to lower the tension level and begin to move things into a more positive gear. So you need to have discussed these techniques in advance and decided on some basic ground rules.

As with all the ideas mentioned in this step, some will work particularly well for you, others won't. So try all of them, at least a few times, experimenting until you find what suits.

Agree a stop signal

Agree between you a code: a word, a phrase, even a gesture that means 'We're starting to fight, so let's stop and look at what's happening'. It needs to be quite unusual so that you won't think it's part of normal conversation. It needs to be friendly rather than confronting, so that it doesn't add to the threatening atmosphere. Some that couples have found useful are: 'Deep water ahead . . .' 'I think we're in trouble here . . .' 'SATBYS' (Stop And Think Before You Speak).

There's a variation on this, called 'crying foul'. In other words, you call to your partner's attention the fact that he or she is not playing fairly, are attacking you or defending themselves, or are otherwise making things worse. This one is best used when you feel you've mastered most of the conflict management techniques, because it does need a great deal of goodwill and co-operation. A partner who copes when it's pointed out that he or she is behaving unhelpfully is a very talented human being indeed!

Bring on a conflict coach

Imagining that someone is witnessing your argument can be enough to get you both acting more positively. Such a 'conflict coach' needs to be a person you respect and admire, someone who'd regard your argument with sympathy but with a 'no-nonsense' attitude. Particularly, he or she needs to be someone who would suggest more helpful ways of behaving. Some conflict coaches that couples have used are: grandma or grandpa, a priest or other religious leader, an older couple with a good relationship. Decide in advance who this person is, then when you feel tension rising between you, say something like: 'Conflict coach time? . . . I think we need the conflict coach in here.' At worst, this should encourage you to both stop and draw breath. At best, it allows you to stand back and together think through some better moves.

Take turns

Taking strict turns to speak not only slows the whole interaction down and so (as mentioned earlier) reduces the tension; it also sets up a structure within which you have to listen to each other, think about what's being said, and respond calmly. It means one person doesn't hog the time and the attention. It means that both of you know you have a chance to make your point. It moves the argument firmly into discussion, and before you know it, you'll be into positive negotiation.

But you do need to keep a careful watch. You need to make sure you're actually taking turns. Many full-grown adults never actually master the art of the two-way conversation, but bicker and fret if they're not actively talking. So try using the 'conch' method. In Golding's novel *The Lord of the Flies*, a group of boys stranded on a desert island tried to maintain their democratic system by means of a conch shell, held by whoever was speaking to make sure everyone else kept quiet and listened. You don't need to use a shell. An ornament, fluffy toy – or the nearest available object on the restaurant table – will do.

Offer personalised comfort

We all need comfort. We particularly need it when feeling threatened to help us feel safe and take the fear away. In a conflict situation, offering comfort can instantly reduce the tension and shift emotional gears: 'When she smiles at me, my whole world lights up. I just can't go on feeling bad.'

But all of us need comfort in the way that's peculiar to us alone. And that may vary dramatically. It's almost as if we each speak a different language. If we're addressed in Greek or Spanish when we only understand English or Italian, then we simply can't respond.

Find out first what your own comfort needs are. If you're not sure what works for you, try remembering how you were given rewards or approval as a child – a hug, an approving word, a loving look, a special treat. The adult variations of these are almost certainly still effective ways of making you feel good – so adapt them to your adult needs.

You also need to know what works for your partner so that you offer the most appropriate comfort possible. You don't want to be rushing off to boil the kettle when what your partner needs is to hear the words 'I love you' – or offering a hug when your partner longs to be left alone to recover. So take the time, outside arguments, to check with each other what some of the possibilities are. Make a list of things that will shift the mood from unhappy to happy. If you're working through this book alone and don't feel you could ask your partner about his or her needs, then notice how he spontaneously offers comfort when you're upset. What someone offers is usually what they need.

Act adult

'Act adult' is based on Transactional Analysis, a psychological method of looking at your words and body language which helps you to spot when you're sliding into unhelpful behaviour, and then to move things back on track.

Briefly, this method asks you to imagine that when you're fighting, each of you is either behaving like a 'rebellious child' or like a 'strict parent'. Neither way of behaving is particularly helpful. The child stirs things up, leaving the other person more annoyed. The parent tries to control, leaving the other person resentful. And whether you have two children, two parents, or one of each in the argument, the result is always painful.

These are some signs that someone is being a 'Rebellious Child':

- talking in a whingey or whiney voice, sulking, shouting.
- demanding: 'I want it . . . it's mine.'
- defending: 'It wasn't my fault . . . I never did anything.'
- blaming: 'I didn't . . . it was your fault . . . you did it.'
- digging heels in, refusing: 'I'm just going to, that's all . . . won't . . . shan't . . . don't want to.'
- playing games: 'I've hidden the scissors . . . you can't have them.'

These are some signs that someone is being a 'Strict Parent':

- talking in a stern cold voice, frowning, looking disapproving and angry.
- criticising: 'You're always late . . . you're so stupid . . . why do you always fail?'
- commanding: 'You must . . . you ought . . . you shouldn't. . . just do as I ask.'
- patronising: 'This is the fifth time I've explained it. I'll go over it once again.'
- justifying: 'I did tell you . . . I knew I was right. . . '
- punishing: 'If you do that again I'll . . . you've been so awful that I'm going to . . .'

A more useful way of behaving is to act like a 'wise adult'. This sort of person would respond to partnership problems in a mature way – reasonable, flexible, relaxed, open to suggestion, and using all available skills to solve the problem. You may notice that this way of behaving is very like the 'win-win' style of conflict mentioned in Step 2.

These are some signs that someone is being a 'Wise Adult':

- talking in a calm, relaxed voice, using open and supportive body language.
- admitting own needs: 'What I'd like is for us to . . . it would really work for me if we . . .'
- not defending own position, feels secure: 'I'm happy to talk about this . . . it's not a problem.'
- accepting the other person's needs: 'I want you to have what you want too.'
- listening: 'I'd like to know how you feel . . . ? I understand what you're saying.'
- negotiating: 'Let's work out what we can do, so that we can both be happy.'

Let's look at what happens when Sam and Megan start a conversation. Megan's feeling very much like a parent at the moment, and Sam is feeling like a child (although on other occasions, during other arguments, they may swap roles with Megan being the child and Sam the parent.)

Sam wants to go along to the quiz night that evening. Megan wants him to spend some time with her.

What happens	What's happening underneath
Sam says in a whingey voice: 'It's a really important match. I want to go.'	He expects her to meet his demands.
Megan says in a cool, critical voice: 'Oh, for heaven's sake. You're always down the pub. I never get to see you when I need to, and I live with you. It's such a stupid game anyway. What on earth do you see in it?'	She criticises him, patronises him, tells him what to do.
Sam says sulkily: 'It's good. I enjoy it. Anyway I missed the last one. You didn't remind me . . .'	He defends himself and blames her.
Megan says sharply: 'I told you they'd changed the time. But did you take any notice? Not you.'	She justifies herself and criticises him.
Sam says stubbornly: 'Well, I'm just going to go. Tough.'	He digs his heels in.
Megan says angrily: 'If you do that, my lad, forget any chance of my giving you a lift down to the match on Saturday.'	She punishes him.

This is the argument from hell. But how could you turn it round? Put simply, transactional analysis suggests that you when you spot that the two of you are acting like this, you simply change your behaviour. Either or both of you can switch to behaving like a 'Wise Adult'. If feelings aren't running too high, you also point out to each other what's happening and suggest that you switch together. Transactional analysis suggests that if just one of you begins to act like this, then the other will slowly but inevitably join in.

What happens if either Sam or Megan switch to 'Wise Adult' mode?

Megan switches to adult mode first.

What happens	What's happening underneath
Sam says in a whingey voice: 'It's a really important match. I want to go.'	He expects her to meet his demands.
Megan says calmly and lovingly, 'It's OK, I understand. It's important to you. I do know that. But I do want us to have some time together tonight: I've got something I really need to talk through with you.'	She bypasses his whinginess and starts to act adult, acknowledges his needs, and states hers clearly.
Sam says in a defensive voice: 'But the match is on tonight.'	He still digs his heels in slightly.
Megan says calmly: 'OK, let's think about this. Don't worry, I'm sure we can work something out. What time does the match finish? Do you need to stay for the whole evening?'	She listens to what he wants, and tries to gain a sense of what's needed.
Sam says in a more reasonable voice: 'It's on at seven, and it should finish about nineish. So maybe I could come straight back afterwards. Would that be OK? What do you need to talk about? Is there a problem at work?'	He now feels much more understood, and is willing to talk about it. He is starting to act adult: listening to her needs and being willing to negotiate.
Megan says calmly: 'No, I'm worried about Kate: she was in a real state when she rang me today.'	She admits her own needs, but doesn't defend her own position, and seems willing to negotiate.
Sam says calmly: 'OK, I'll be back at about nine-fifteen and we'll talk about it then.'	He responds and meets her needs.

Here, Sam switches to adult mode first.

What happens	What's happening underneath
Sam says in a whingey voice: 'It's a really important match. I want to go.'	He expects her to meet his demands.
Megan says in a cool critical voice: 'Oh, for heaven's sake. I never get to see you, when I need to. It's such a stupid game anyway. What on earth do you see in it? '	She criticises him, patronises him, tells him what to do.
Sam says calmly: 'Oh, right. Tell me about needing to see me. Is there something particular you want to talk about?'	He bypasses her criticisms. and starts to act adult, listens and accepts her needs.
Megan says in a more reasonable voice: 'Well . . . yes, I'm worried about Kate: she was in a real state when she rang me today.'	She starts to feel more understood, and is willing to admit what she needs.
Sam says in a calm voice: 'OK, I understand that. I really want to go to the match and it starts at seven. But it finishes around nineish. Why don't we spend some time now talking. Then if we haven't quite sorted things, I'll come home right after the match.'	He admits his own needs, but doesn't defend his own position and is willing to negotiate.
Megan says happily: 'That sounds great. If we don't finish up now, stay and have a pint. I'm sure if you're back by ten we can sort it out tonight.'	She starts to become willing to meet his needs and negotiate.

In both scenarios, just the fact that one partner behaved more like an adult had an effect. It took a few moments for the other partner to shift gear too, but it happened. By moving things to a more equal level – rather than each partner wanting control – the whole thing lost its sense of conflict and turned into real co-operation.

Take time out

What if things seem out of hand? If things feel far too emotional, or seem a bit out of order, you need to know you can handle that. One good way to be sure is to use 'time out', a system developed by John Gottman, an American psychologist.

Decide together, ahead of time, on a code word or phrase. One of you can use this if you start to feel seriously uncomfortable or threatened emotionally or physically: 'We need to stop I mean it. We need to take a break.' Even if the other of you is feeling fine, this code needs to be honoured.

When the code word is used during an argument, that's the signal that you're going to spend a period apart. To calm down emotionally you should take a minimum of twenty minutes, but you may want to spend longer apart to order your thoughts. This time apart isn't, though, an excuse not to deal with the original problem, or a way that one of you can simply call a halt to any interaction and retreat. So you should also agree exactly when you'll come back together and start talking again more positively.

Use the time apart to focus on what's been happening. Try to understand why you were arguing. Particularly and most importantly, try to realise what's been happening for your partner, what their fears are, what their emotions are trying to tell them.

Come back together at the time agreed. Bring your realisations back with you, and use them to move the discussion on to a more positive level.

! ══════════════ *Task 6.3* ══════════════

Driving lesson – Part two

NB: This is a task to do only if you can swap notes with your partner.

Sit down together and think back over the strategies you need to use together. Decide on just one which you could use next time you feel yourselves sliding into an argument. Agree ahead of time how you'll remind each other to use this strategy.

(Forward to Step 10, page 183)

!

HOW DO YOU KNOW WHEN
_____IT'S OVER?_____

*'We're real drama queens, even after so many decades together.
If we start a fight, it's screaming and shouting all over the
place, with her sobbing in the bedroom and me storming up and
down the hall. Then again, we're also very good at the making-up
bit. There's a real feeling of victory that we've turned it round and
we now feel good about each other. We'll cry and hug, and usually
make love, wherever we are, if it's not public. So if we argue for an
hour, we walk round on air for a day feeling happy. Also, there is a
sense, if we argue, that the whole thing might get out of control
and we might split up like we did four years ago. Neither of us
would ever want that to happen again. So when we make up,
there's always a feeling of danger averted.'*   Len

Slowly but surely, bit by bit, you've turned the argument round.
You've lowered the painful feeling. You've recovered the good
feeling. You're both talking rather than shouting, discussing
rather than arguing.

These are twelve signals that things are turning round. When
you see them or hear them, you know that you're bringing the
relationship back to balance. Whatever it is you've been doing –
listening, smiling, co-operating, comforting – do it some more,
because it obviously works.

Your inner emotional signals:

- You start thinking positively about your partner and what he
  or she is doing.
- You feel general and personalised signals of relaxation and
  satisfaction, for example, relaxed stomach, chest or back
  muscles.
- You start thinking that it was crazy or stupid to argue.
- You start being able to admit, at least to yourself, your part in
  the argument.
- You start thinking about and maybe even mentioning to your
  partner, good times you've shared in the past or hopes you
  have for the future.

Signals between you:

- You talk as much as you usually do.
- You can look at each other again.
- You can hear your partner's voice without tensing, because he or she is relaxed and normal.
- You check with each other: 'Are you OK now? Are you feeling better?' and receive a genuinely enthusiastic response.
- You use agreement phrases: 'Yes . . . Let's do that . . . Fine by me' – and they're genuine.
- You use acknowledgement phrases: 'I see what you mean . . . I know you feel like that.'
- You use permission phrases: 'Of course you can . . . Whatever you want to do is fine by me.'
- You can touch each other again as much as you normally do.

Of course, these signals are only a sign that good feeling is restored. And sometimes this is all you need to do. Sometimes the main thing that's responsible for your quarrel isn't a specific issue, but stress and tension, built-up bad feeling, or a simple lack of skill and practice in conflict management. Particularly if your argument was triggered by lifestyle issues, and the message your feelings gave you was simply 'relax more . . . be more intimate . . . you're overworking . . .', then once the emotions have faded, the conflict is over.

But often, there are issues that need sorting. The skills for how to do this – by communication and negotiation – are what you'll learn in the next two steps. When to do this? You may want to go on immediately, but it's also fine to leave a gap between the end of the argument and the start of the problem-solving. Agree between you a time and space when you'll resolve things: this evening when the kids are in bed, next weekend when you're away. Then stick to this agreement. If you don't, be warned: the arguments will start all over again. (If they do, then use Relax, Review and Reach Out to move things back on track again, and make sure that this time, you do sort things out.)

It's a good idea, though, whether or not the issue itself has been resolved, to mark the point when the bad feeling stops. Don't just drift off in separate directions, to mow the lawn or make the lunch. You spend time together unhappily to fight. Why not spend time together happily to celebrate that you've stopped fighting, to make a statement that you feel good about each other again?

You might have a hug. You might have sex. You might have a cup of coffee and a biscuit, or go out for a slap-up meal. You might take a walk together or simply watch your favourite sitcom, cuddled up in each other's arms.

You both need time, time to recover: bad feeling takes it out of you mentally and physically. Time to rediscover trust: you may still be a bit shaken by what's happened. Time to get back in tune so that you can face the world together. Give yourselves that time, because you deserve it.

But then, let the whole thing go. Don't rake up the bad feeling that evening, tomorrow, next month. Don't remind yourselves, or each other, that you behaved badly. Of course, remember to resolve the issues. But make a point of forgetting the fight. When it comes to conflict, amnesia is a very useful tool.

WHERE ARE YOU NOW?

Step 6 has helped you to see your arguments from the outside, to begin to learn to take charge, and to do things to turn them in a positive direction.

As you complete the tasks in this step, remember to turn to Step 10 on page 183 and fill in the relevant sections there.

Move on to Step 7 when:

- you know you're beginning to spot arguments ahead of time.

- you're able to use Relax, Review and Reach Out to choose what to do next.

- you're beginning to use a range of strategies to drive your arguments positively.

START COMMUNICATING

'Rob's in the merchant navy, and can be away for months at a time. It's hard being apart. But one thing that does work for us is that we know we have to talk when he comes home, otherwise we lose it totally. It's a bit like being away on a secret service mission: you have to debrief when you get back. If we don't, we just find we're totally out of sync, and trip each other up about everything. So I'll take time off work, we'll take a day or two just on our own. We'll send the kids off to grandma's, stay in bed most of the time, and literally talk through everything that's happened, everything we've thought and felt. We do talk well, and we do listen well. I think that's the only thing that's kept us together.' Karen

Most times, stopping the arguments is only the beginning. Most arguments happen for a reason: there's an issue to resolve and a need to be met. It may be tiny: you consistently leave the fridge door open and your partner objects. It may be huge: your partner has sexual fantasies that you deeply object to. It may be fundamental: the fact that you rarely talk to each other means that you feel devalued in the relationship. And if you want to approach the problem in a win-win style, it isn't enough just to feel good. You have to start communicating with each other in order to start seeing results. You have to start communicating in order to make sure that bad feeling doesn't build up, and lead to yet more arguments.

Here are ten specific ways in which you can use communication to avoid conflict:

- by touching base on a day-to-day basis and so becoming closer
- by helping you understand each other's differences
- by sharing emotions and so defusing arguments

- by updating each other on ways in which life changes have shifted your expectations
- by exchanging information on your individual needs
- by making arrangements to cope with practical problems
- by defusing tension as it rises
- by trouble-shooting problems in advance
- by preparing the ground for negotiation on specific issues
- by increasing your trust that problems will be resolved eventually.

You may feel that you already do communicate with each other – you talk all the time. But just as we're hardly ever taught how to resolve a conflict, so we're hardly ever taught to communicate effectively. This step teaches the basic of truly deep communication: the sort that goes beyond checking out if you've bought the bread, or deciding what to watch on television tonight.

First, a warning. Don't try to use this sort of communication if you find the bad feeling rising again. Bad feeling, if you remember, creates hearing loss. So if you feel a build-up of wariness or irritation, fear or fury, then go back to what you've learned earlier in this book about handling your emotions and driving an argument. Use those techniques to calm your feelings and register the message they're giving you. Only then carry on exchanging information and gaining insight in the ways suggested in this step.

! ══════════ *Task 7.1* ══════════

Communication practice

NB: This is a task to do only if you can swap notes with your partner.

Start setting aside time to practise communicating, at least once a week.

Take about five minutes each, in turn, to talk about what you think and feel. Start with safe topics, but if you seem to be doing well, then after ten or a dozen sessions, you can start talking about your relationship.

The partner not talking should simply stay silent and listen. Afterwards, separate. Go and do something else for a while, so that you have time to think about what you've both said.

Don't use these conversations as ammunition during quarrels at a latter date.

(Forward to Step 10, page 183)   !

HOW TO LISTEN WITH AN
OPEN MIND

'I remember that when we first started going out, she was very hesitant about sex. She'd go so far and then pull back. We went on like this for weeks and I was beginning to wonder whether there was any point in going on. Then one day we were walking in the woods and she started to tell me what had happened with her first husband, how badly he'd treated her, in bed and out of it. Once she'd started, the flood gates opened and she just didn't stop talking, for hours. It took a while longer before things fell into place, but she says now that it was what happened in the woods that made her feel that it was OK to trust me.'   Jack

The first foundation stone in communication is listening. And the first stage of that is learning to listen not only with your ears, but with your mind too.

For while your partner is talking, it's as vital not to converse in your head as it is not to talk with your mouth. If you keep thinking your own thoughts, then you can't listen to your partner's perceptions. If you're only aware of your own feelings, then you can't empathise with your partner's emotions.

So once your partner begins speaking, ignore what's going on in your head. Simply focus all your attention on his or her words – focusing your actual eye gaze can help you do this – and ignore any inner 'static'. If you do find yourself drifting away – maybe comparing your partner's experience with your own, or rehearsing your words for when your turn comes – tune in again to your partner's insights and tune out from your own.

Also, try to avoid mental criticism. For however hard you've both worked to reduce the previous bad feeling and reach a point where you can communicate, if you then start from a critical mindset, communication won't be positive or effective. Particularly, try to avoid these types of critical thought:

- Listening from the start with an expectation that your partner will repeat old habits: 'I bet he's going to drag up that old resentment about . . . I've heard it all before . . . She'll say good things but she won't mean them . . .'

- Judging your partner's ideas mentally without giving him a chance to explain those ideas to you: 'That's a terrible idea she's had ... Oh no, he's not suggesting that, is he ...?'
- Setting up stringent mental conditions on what is acceptable so that you don't even consider most of your partner's suggestions: 'Well, I'm not having that . . . That's out for a start ...'

This kind of mental negativity not only makes it very difficult for you to have a fair and reasonable communication – you've already set up blocks against what your partner is saying. It also has an unfortunate effect on your partner.

It tells him or her that you're not open to any point of view other than your own. And it does that silently, and without you even knowing. For as you listen, your body language unconsciously reflects your thoughts, and there's very little you can do about that. Your posture, the way your eyes move, the twist of your mouth or the shrug of your shoulders, can signal all too well whether you're interested, positive and supportive, or bored, critical and judgmental. Which message do you want your partner to receive? If it's the positive one, then keeping an open mind will ensure that your body language signals receptivity.

The real point of keeping an 'open' mind may only be apparent when you're at the receiving end, when your partner listens to you openly and with interest. Then, you'll be amazed at how much more relaxed you feel, how much more trusting, how much more loved. You'll also be amazed at how much that seems to affect your dynamic, how much more you can accept each other, and how much easier it is to reach agreement. Deep communication does begin in the mind, rather than with the words.

REFLECT YOUR PARTNER'S VALUE

As well as being listened to, everyone also wants to be appreciated. If you show your partner that what he or she is trying to communicate is important and valuable to you, you increase the chances both of your being able to communicate more clearly, and of your partner's responding in kind.

Here Lindsay has something important to communicate to her partner Paul. She wants to go and visit her mum, who has been ill.

What happens	What's happening underneath
Lindsay says: 'Can we talk about visiting my mum this weekend?'	She's feeling worried.
Paul says, distractedly: 'Yeah, sure love . . . this film's great.'	He keeps looking at the television.
Lindsay says in a worried voice: 'Paul, listen. I want to visit my mum. She's not at all well.'	She's not feeling listened to.
Paul says smilingly: 'Come on, she's not at death's door.'	He mocks her feelings because he doesn't take her seriously.
Lindsay says defensively: 'I know, but I do worry that–'	She knows she's not being taken seriously.
Paul says: 'Calm down, love. If you want my opinion, you're worrying for nothing.'	He interrupts her, and then trivialises what she's saying.
Lindsay says: ' I do worry. I can't help remembering when my Dad died. I should've been there.'	She feels cut across, and belittled.
Paul says: 'Yes, but your Dad had cancer. This isn't the same.'	He puts forward his opinion as more correct than hers.
Lindsay says nothing.	She's really thinking: 'That's not the point. I want to go and see her.'
Paul says dismissively: 'I just know there's no problem. So there's no need to go up – OK?'	He feels he's proved his point, so closes the discussion.
Lindsay says nothing.	She's really thinking: 'Oh, why bother?'

It's clear just where Paul went wrong. His body language was incredibly off-putting. He wasn't respectful of what Lindsay said. He interrupted her, cut across her, and gave her no real chance to communicate what she was feeling. All in all, he rode rough shod over what she needed.

Let's replay that more positively.

What happens	What's happening underneath
Lindsay says 'Can we talk about visiting my mum this weekend?'	She's feeling worried.
Paul says neutrally: 'Hold on, love. I'll turn this film off. Now, about going up to your mum's.'	He deals with the distraction, then brings the conversation back to her making it clear that he's prepared to listen.
Lindsay says: 'She's not at all well.'	She feels listened to.
Paul says seriously: 'I know you're worried.'	He doesn't necessarily agree with her, but he acknowledges her point of view.
Lindsay says: 'I can't help remembering when Dad died. I should've been there.'	She thinks: 'He's taking me seriously.'
Paul says: 'You were ever so upset about that. It's not surprising you're worried now.'	He thinks: 'It's her mum – she has to play this the way she wants.' He acknowledges her opinion.
Lindsay says: 'So should we go up there?'	She feels understood.
Paul: 'I'm not as worried as you are about your mum so I don't particularly want to go up this weekend. But you're worried. So let's work out what to do. Could you go up on your own?'	He states his point of view, but still acknowledges hers.
Lindsay says: 'OK, I'll do that.'	She thinks, 'That's fair . . .'

Paul doesn't ignore his own thoughts, beliefs, feelings or needs. He doesn't agree with Lindsay just to keep her happy. But he does concentrate on what she's saying and does show her that he's listening. He also shows he respects her views and feelings, that he wants to talk about things, that he wants to meet her needs as well as his.

What Paul and Lindsay show us is that, as you listen . . .

- Rather than taking attention away from your partner, ride out interruptions then bring things gently back to the point they were beforehand.
- Rather than using unappreciative body language, turn towards your partner, look at him, offer appreciation in the form of touch.
- Rather than mocking, either by what you say or by your expression, show respect. Particularly beware sarcasm, which is not only mocking but often cruelly so.
- Rather than interrupting, wait for your partner to finish speaking before you speak.
- Rather than giving your own opinion or advice too early, wait until your partner feels you've really understood what she is saying, and then offer your thoughts as just one possibility. Particularly beware 'yes, but'.
- Rather than arguing, intellectualising or proving your point, acknowledge your partner's point. You may not agree, but your partner has a right to his thoughts and feelings.

ARE YOU HEARING WHAT YOUR PARTNER IS SAYING?

If you listen well, your partner will feel unthreatened. He (or she) will be relaxed and able to open up to you. And then you can start to learn what he thinks, what he needs. You can make sure you're hearing what's actually being said.

The first secret here is to listen not only to the words. For what your partner is actually saying is only a very small proportion of his story: some estimates say that over 90 per cent of communication is actually done not through language but through body language. So watch out for non-verbal signs that show something is important, such as extra stress on a word, a pause before it, or a shift in voice tone. Watch out for signs that your partner feels bad: a raised voice tone, a frown or a long troubled silence. If there's something he doesn't want to say, he may bite his lip or put his hand to his mouth. If he's trying to please, but

.underneath is frightened of your reaction, he may smile but the smile may not reach his eyes.

Next, listen to what your partner is saying, though be aware that his words are only the tip of the iceberg. Remember that he may be talking about what's happening now, but thinking back to an unhappy memory. He may be describing events, but be holding back on emotions. He may be talking about surface topics, but be pleading for underlying needs to be met. He may be speaking generally, but have a particular example of something in mind.

Particularly, avoid 'mind reading', jumping to conclusions about your partner's thoughts and feelings. This doesn't only mean the sort of pessimistic interpretation mentioned earlier which characterises couples far down the Disillusionment Path. Even when you're both content with each other, you can totally misunderstand what is wanted, or presume what is expected.

Donald always thought that if his wife stayed downstairs to watch television after he went up to bed, that meant she was angry with him, until he discovered that it was linked with her having a bad day with the kids and needing extra 'time to wind down'. If you find yourself thinking things like 'I'm sure he wants me to . . . He probably feels . . . His expression means that he feels bad about . . . ', then you may be mind reading. Don't take anything for granted.

So make sure you really understand. Explore the issues in more detail. Sort out assumptions. Say things like 'Tell me that again, but in a bit more detail', 'What did you feel when that happened?', 'Does this remind you of anything else that's ever happened to you?', 'Can you give me some examples of times when . . .' Particularly, make sure that if your partner expresses a need, you've understood exactly what that need is, because meeting it will be the key to resolving the issue between you.

The best way to find out whether you've truly understood your partner is to tell him what you think you've heard. When he pauses, repeat back what was said, not word for word, but your understanding of his thoughts and feelings, perhaps ending with 'Is that what you really meant?'.

This will not only give your partner the chance to tell you if you've misunderstood him. It will also fix in your mind more clearly just what it is your partner thinks, feels – and means.

!═══════════════ *Task 7.2* ═══════════════

Listening practice

On three occasions in the next week, during the course of normal conversation, listen to your partner. Choose times when your partner is talking about something that isn't upsetting to you.

Listen with an open mind. Show your partner that his or her communication is valuable. Make sure you're hearing what's being said.

What effect does doing this have on you? On your partner? Practise this skill as often as you can.

(Forward to Step 10, page 183)

!

TALKING TO MAKE CONTACT

'I like the fact that she confides in me. I certainly didn't have that with my wife. We just got on with things, and kept a stiff upper lip. But with 'Cesca I get everything while we're having tea: what's happened at the shop, what her friends said, what she's happy about, how her HRT's affecting her! It can be too much, like a flood sometimes. But I never ask her to leave it for another day. It's the first time in my life I've felt included, trusted – loved – and I don't intend to throw all that away.'   Tony

There are ways of talking which, frankly, make it hard for any listener to concentrate, appreciate or understand. But there are also ways of talking that mean other people listen. To make real contact, to help your partner take in what you're saying, use that second approach.

Set the scene

The right setting makes talking (and listening) easier. So choose a private space with no interruptions or distractions, well away from the phone, the dog or the children. Set aside time that's yours, where you're not going to be interrupted: half an hour or an hour during a quiet evening, not five minutes just as the children are coming in from school. Make sure you're both calm, not too tired, and clear headed. And don't even think of starting a useful discussion at the end of a stressed-out evening when you've both had a few drinks.

Engage

It can be tempting to hold back when talking to your partner. Particularly if you're sharing needs that you fear your partner will object to, you may be wary of opening up. But confiding is one of the most powerful ways to build your relationship. So involve your partner in what you're saying. Use your words to make mental and emotional contact. And use your body language to make physical contact: turn towards your partner, look at him or her, touch him if you're both 'touchy' people.

If you feel yourself falling silent or holding back, change your approach. Instead of talking about the issue you're discussing, switch to talking about what you're feeling right now. 'I feel scared that I might hurt you . . . I'm starting to feel nervous now . . . I feel I don't know what to say next . . .'. By bringing into the open what's happening right here and right now, you'll often find that your inhibition disappears and you can carry on talking about the original topic.

A particular challenge is where there are 'no-go' areas in your relationship, issues that always lead to arguments because they're so painful. If you have these in your relationship, then remember to go back to Steps 4 and 5 and deal with the uncomfortable emotion before you try to communicate.

Don't hog the limelight

If holding back is a temptation, then so is holding forth. It's not as important to take turns when you're just chatting. But when the topic is vital – your relationship and the issues surrounding it – then your partner will take in more and sympathise more if you don't monopolise the conversation. So talk in bite-sized chunks, several sentences rather than several minutes at a time, so that your partner doesn't faze out. Give your partner a chance to speak when your views have had reasonable time and space. And if what you're saying seems to leave your partner upset or irritated, stop and check that out. You'll gain a better hearing if you do.

Be co-operative rather than combative

Even when you aren't attacking or defending, there are ways of communicating that can challenge rather than support, that can be combative rather than co-operative. Avoid these like the plague; they will mysteriously slide the conversation back into the war zone. Instead, try communicating in ways that show that you accept your partner's point of view, want to find ways of resolving your differences, and don't simply expect (or demand) that they will fall in with your way of thinking.

Ian and Maureen are discussing what to buy Maureen's son for his birthday.

Accept suggestions rather than dismissing ideas out of hand.

M: 'Should we take him to a theme park for the day?'

This response wouldn't help:

I: 'Absolutely not. Total waste of money.' This is very dismissive. Maureen then feels put down and will react accordingly.

This response would mean things went more easily:

I: 'I'm a bit concerned about the cash. Let's see if we can make the money side of it work.' This expresses his worries, but is more likely to lead to a solution.

Stress similarities between you rather than pointing out differences.

M: 'I think he's old enough to have a proper two-wheeled bike.'

This response wouldn't help:

I: 'No, he won't be ready for one of those for ages!' This simply contradicts what Maureen has said, and so turns communication into conflict.

This response would mean things went more easily:

I: 'Yes, I agree with you he should have a bike. Let's talk about when it will be the right time for one.' This leads on to a discussion.

Make requests rather than giving commands.

M: 'OK, we've decided on the computer, then.'

This response wouldn't help:

I: 'Well, I'm far too busy this week. You'll just have to pick it up next time you're in town.' Maureen is likely to react badly to being ordered around.

This response would mean things went more easily:

I: 'I'm so busy this week. Is there any possibility you could pick it up next time you're in town?' Maureen is likely to respond better to a request.

Stay on track rather than wandering off it

Communication always works better when it's focused. Particularly when you're discussing an issue that needs resolving, you'll gain better results if you concentrate on that issue rather than wandering off on to others. Of course, it can be tempting, particularly if you both have a backlog of grievances built up, to seize any chance of talking together as a chance to air your worries. It's always better to stick with the problem in hand, and save others for another day.

Focus your talk rather than opening a window of opportunity on to other resentments.

Maddie and Les are discussing the fact that the car needs mending.

L: 'It's a real shame that this has come up now. Just when I thought I was going to have a free weekend.'

This response wouldn't help:

M: 'Yes, and what about all this stuff you've been promising to do around the house. Shall I get you the list?' This leads them off track.

This response would mean things went more easily:

M: 'Yes, it's a real problem. How can we get it done quickly so you can have a bit of time off?' This keeps them on track.

Stay with the present communication rather than going back to past problems.

M: 'Perhaps if we asked Barbara's husband, Frank, to give you a hand.'

This response wouldn't help:

L: 'Yes, but you know what happened last time . . . it took for ever. I wish you wouldn't ask him.' This leads them off track.

This response would mean things went more easily:

L: ' I'd rather do it myself. I feel more in control when I do the whole job.' This keeps them on track.

Be straight rather than curved

If you want to make your point clearly, you have to say what you mean. This doesn't mean aggressively, but being honest and courageous rather than letting yourself bend the truth because you're nervous, or afraid of your partner's reaction. This can be hard, especially if a certain issue has become such a 'no-go area' between you that if one mentions it, the other immediately goes on the defence. But if you aren't honest about what you think, feel and need, your partner has no chance of responding honestly – and no chance of taking action.

Use direct statements rather than using indirect ones.

Harry and Dot are talking about their grandson's wedding.

D: 'What are you going to wear?'

This response wouldn't help:

H: 'No one'll mind if I don't wear the full top-hat bit, will they? Dot will then tell Harry just who *will* mind, which isn't the point he's making.

This response might seem uncomfortably direct, but would mean things went more easily in the long term:

H: 'I'd feel much better not wearing the full-top hat bit.' They can now talk about what Harry feels and wants.

Speak directly about what bothers you rather than changing the subject or turning things into a joke.

H: 'Well, at least it'll be nice to meet up with all the old crowd the night before. We'll have a laugh.'

This response wouldn't help:

D: 'Mmmmm. What time do we have to be there?' She changes the subject, which means that her concern about going has less chance of being dealt with.

This response wouldn't help either:

D: 'Old crowd is right – I'll be the baby – I might give it a miss!' She makes a joke, hiding the fact that she doesn't want to go.

This response might seem uncomfortably direct, but would mean things went more easily in the long term:

D: 'Is it all right if I don't come with you the night before? I've never got really on with that crowd. I'd much rather stay at home and get ready for the big day.' She brings the issue out so that they can deal with it.

Talk about the issue that's a problem, rather than about the one that isn't.

H: 'I'm so looking forward to the wedding.'

This response wouldn't help:

D: 'But your sister'll keep asking me when Fiona's going to get pregnant, and your brother'll keep telling me how well his eldest is doing.' In reply to this Harry will offer practical suggestions for how to cope, which won't help solve Dot's real problem.

This response might seem uncomfortably direct, but would mean things went more easily in the long term:

D: 'I feel when I'm with your family that they think we've been awful parents and failures in life. When we're with them, I'd

like you to show how proud you are of me and our children.'
They can now discuss how Harry could support Dot more and
show that he values her.

Say what the problem is rather than denying it.

D: 'I'd love to have a new dress, but can we afford it?'

This response wouldn't help:

H: 'Of course we can, love.' Money is tight, so agreeing to Dot's
request will actually create problems in the long term.

This response might seem uncomfortably direct, but would mean
things went more easily:

H: 'I'm not sure. I want you to have whatever you want, but I am
worried about the money. How much d'you think it'll cost?'
Admitting the problem means they can deal with it.

! ═══════════════ *Task 7.3* ═══════════════

Talking practice

On three occasions in the next week, in the course of normal conversation, use at least one talking skill you've learned in this step. Make
sure you're not talking about something that might upset your partner.

Engage. Don't hog the limelight. Be co-operative rather than
combative. Stay on track. Be straight rather than curved.

What effect does doing these things have on you? On your partner?
Practise this skill as often as you can.

(**Forward to Step 10**, page 183)   **!**

DID YOU SAY WHAT I THINK
YOU SAID?

You listen well. You talk well. There's good feeling between you.
But in the end, you still may not have actually communicated. So
it's vital to keep checking this. When you're talking and your
partner is listening, challenge misunderstandings. Notice if she (or
he) is using inappropriate body language, has a vague expression

or distracted movements. Notice if her comments about what you say are confused or irrelevant. If you don't feel she's understood you, say so. Then try repeating what you've said. Make your points differently. Give new examples. Keep going until you know your partner's fully understood.

At the same time, let your partner check that you've understood what he (or she) said. Repeat back what you think you've heard, as suggested earlier, so your partner can tell you if you've heard correctly. If he's talking, occasionally ask: 'Do you feel I understood you? . . . Do you feel I heard what you said?'

This isn't to say that you have to agree with your partner: you don't. Good listening is about allowing the other person his or her opinion, not surrendering your own. But taking the time to check that your partner feels that you've listened will reassure him that you're committed to doing so. And if he thinks you've not grasped what he's trying to say, don't feel threatened. Instead, put your energy into listening more, and at a deeper level.

Good listening is about allowing the other person their opinion, not surrendering your own.

A final idea is to compare notes regularly, at points during your discussion. Particularly if you're resolving an issue, stop at intervals to reach agreement on what each of you thinks has been decided so far. A good formula is: 'You think . . . I think . . . We agree . . . We're going to . . .'

'You think that Liam's not doing well at school. I think he seems happy even if he's not doing well in exams. We agreed we need to talk to him and to his teacher. We're going to sit down and chat when he comes in tonight, and I'm going to ring the school and make an appointment.'

If you want to keep conflict at bay, you need to keep communicating regularly. You need to talk every day, not just in passing but in a way that allows each of you to know the other more and more intimately. If you don't, then slowly, but inevitably, bad feeling will start to creep in. If you do, then just as inevitably but rather more quickly, good feeling will build up. For couples who communicate and keep communicating seem to develop a store of relationship resilience. They can disagree, and not mind. They can hit difficulties and overcome them. They can feel battered by outside circumstances, and still survive.

WHERE ARE YOU NOW?

Step 7 has helped you develop your communication skills, so that you begin to talk through issues with your partner in a way that helps both of you.

As you complete the tasks in this step, remember to turn to Step 10 on page 183 and fill in the relevant sections there.

Move on to Step 8 when:

- you're communicating with your partner about thoughts and feelings regularly. (If you're working through the book alone, allow yourself extra time so that what you're doing encourages your partner to start to communicate too.)

- you feel you can listen well to your partner the majority of the time.

- you feel that you're able to talk to your partner in a way that helps him or her to listen.

RESOLVE THE ISSUE

'We've been together now for nearly twenty-two years. And yes, of course we argue. But I don't think either of us has ever argued the other into the ground. What I mean is this. I remember we were on holiday on the Isle of Wight once, and in the B and B we shared a table with a couple from up north. Every night, we'd talk about something. And every night, he had to win out. It didn't matter what it was – what they were going to eat, what they were doing next day, what presents they were going to buy for the grandchildren – he would always have his own way. She never gave her side of things. She kept smiling, but she wasn't a happy woman.'

Pete

While communication will move you on, often it doesn't let you reach your destination. So although unclear expectations may be sorted out simply by talking about them, some of the time even once they're understood, you may be left unhappy. And while a decision may be discussed for days, in the end, none of the options leave you satisfied. You need to resolve the issue.

All this may seem difficult. It may seem particularly hard if the main issue that needs sorting out between you both is a long-standing one. An affair, a money decision that went badly, a source of daily resentment. These things may have become 'no-go' areas that the two of you can't even talk about, as was the case with Marion, who tried and failed to persuade her husband not to send their children away to boarding school, and said she still felt bitter about it at the time her grandchildren were born. So if you have such an issue, reduce the bad feeling before you start to resolve it, by using the suggestions made in Steps 4 and 5.

The prospect of sorting out issues between you may also seem difficult if your partner doesn't seem motivated to join in – especially if you're working through this book alone. But there's still a lot you can alone do to make a start. And if one of you starts using the techniques outlined in this step, it will make it easier for the other to follow. Short term, of course, there may be no reciprocation. But if one of you does make a move, then perhaps not the first time this happens, nor the second, nor the fifth, but eventually, your partner will almost certainly start to do the same. In the end, you'll both have more of what you want.

WHAT DO YOU NEED?

'We went for a walk down by the canal, Myles asked me to marry him, and then he presented me with a ring. I was so happy I cried, until I opened the box. The ring was awful: old and ugly and not what I'd imagined at all. I threw it at him and stormed off. I cringe to think of it now. He caught up with me, and we sat in the car and talked. The ring was his grandmother's, a family heirloom, and he'd given it to me because it was special. Once he'd explained that, I realised that what I really wanted was the ring that he wanted to give me. In the end, its significance meant so much more to me than the pretty diamond sparkle I'd always thought was important.'

Susan

You have to start any resolution process with sorting out what you personally want: not because it's the most important thing, but because until you do, you can't successfully ask for it or negotiate for it.

What Susan realised was that what she thought she wanted wasn't what she actually wanted at all. When it came down to it, the pretty ring she'd always dreamed of wasn't the crucial issue. It was the sentiment, the emotion, the statement Myles made by giving her his grandmother's ring that was the important thing. She'd thought that diamonds and gold were what would prove Myles loved her. In the end, the giving of his grandmother's ring was a far more powerful statement of love for her.

Like Susan, you may be unclear about what you want, and not realise it. One reason for this is that all of us are told so often, as we grow up, that our needs aren't important and that we don't deserve to have them met. In fact, this is a myth. Needs – for big things like love and success, or tiny things like a hug or a kind

> **If you don't know what you want, it's very difficult to go and get it.**

word – are a vital part of being human. We have every right to fulfil them.

But if you feel that having needs and meeting them isn't acceptable, then you may not be aware of what you truly need. Therefore, you may not be able to meet those needs. If you don't know what you want, it's very difficult for you to go and get it.

Try using this seven-stage process to help you think through what it is that you want.

1 Make a first guess

You want a ring, you want a weekend away, you want your partner to listen to you more. What's your first guess about what you want?

2 Be positive

If you only say what you don't want, it's much more difficult for other people to do what you want. So rather than telling your partner to stop waking you as she tumbles out of bed noisily every morning, ask her to get up and go downstairs quietly.

3 Discover the real need

Find out what needs lie behind what you want and you've a much better chance of being satisfied. (The surface issue may be household finances, baby-sitting or who takes the lead in bed . . . but underneath all that there'll be a deeper demand.) Do you want to know that you're respected, to know that the family is secure, to know that you can get what you want in your relationship? Especially, find out whether your real need is a Fundamental Need: value, control or success. If, like Susan, your real need is much deeper than you realise, then having only the surface need met may not actually satisfy you. And if, as she did, you can acknowledge that your real need may be better satisfied by something that your partner wants to give you, then recognizing your real need may provide the resolution to your issue.

4   *Specify the evidence*

Make sure that your partner doesn't misunderstand what evidence of meeting this real need would be. Each of us has our own definition of what things such as respect, security, freedom, affection, value, control and success really mean. And this can lead to a lot of confusion and upset. Susan's original disappointment over the ring that Myles offered her could have been avoided had he known that, for her, evidence of love was gold and set with diamonds. (In fact, they found another solution to their problem.) But if you catch yourself expressing your needs in general terms such as 'I need to know you're loyal to me . . .', stop, redefine your terms specifically, then make sure your partner understands exactly what you mean.

5   *Admit what isn't important*

There may be some parts of what you want that you can do without, or replace. Susan thought she wanted a diamond ring, but in the end, the diamonds were unnecessary. You may want a weekend away, but whether it's in a caravan, a hotel or a tent may be irrelevant.

6   *Be realistic*

Don't ask for the impossible: your partner can choose to be on time or to lose weight, but she can't choose to be five foot nine when she is five foot two. Don't ask for the unthinkable: some things may be possible for your partner but, in their eyes, be immoral, indecent or just plain wrong. And don't ask for the moon: Fundamental Needs in particular simply can't be met completely by another human being. However much your partner cares for you, she can't make you feel totally loved, utterly in control or completely fulfilled all the time. Only you can do this for yourself.

7   *Be clear about the bottom line*

Work out just what the consequences will be if you don't have your needs met. If you know that even if you don't have what you want over a particular issue, you'll still stay in your relationship, then you shouldn't cry 'wolf' and threaten to leave just in order to have your own way. So if having children is important to you, but you'll stick with the relationship even if your partner can't oblige, then reassure her. On the other hand, if you know that something isn't acceptable, it's clearer and fairer all round to say so. So if your partner wants to have an affair and you know you can't be in a relationship that includes a third person, tell him.

! ═══════════ *Task 8.1* ═══════════

Have what you want

Some time during the next week, give yourself a treat: maybe something you've wanted for a long time, or maybe something quite day-to-day, such as an evening in with a good video.

There are only two rules. First, make sure that you're giving yourself something you truly want. Second, make sure that in the process, you don't take anything away from your partner. Enjoy yourself.

(Forward to Step 10, page 183)

!

CRUNCH POINT: WHO AND WHAT COMES FIRST?

'Once we moved in together, she became restless. She was out a lot, I stayed in, we had different friends. We were living different lives, and not willing to bring those lives together. It came to a head when she wanted us to move house, said that might save the relationship. And I realised that actually, what she wanted wasn't important to me any more. We split up for eighteen months, and met again two years ago. We'd both changed, grown up. Now we're working as a unit, we do things together we consider each other. Particularly since Daniel was born, we realise that we're interdependent. I'm not happy if she's not. And I know she feels the same.' Richard

The second essential to resolving the issue is to accept a basic bottom line, which is this. Both of you have an equal right to what you want. For even if your partner's needs are different from yours, it doesn't mean to say that they're less worthwhile.

Nowadays, it's very easy to see every issue in terms of win and lose. Present-day living, with its emphasis on the individual, means that we feel bad if we don't win out. It isn't just that we aren't getting the goodies. It's that we may be seen as failures, that we may come across as weak, bad or unsuccessful if we give ground to anyone else over anything. At the end of the twentieth century, surely only losers don't 'have it all'.

It doesn't work like that in love. In relationships, you need win-win solutions, the end point of win-win styles of conflict management. For if you go for what you alone want, and ignore what your partner wants, you end up with an imbalance that will create regular conflict. If you hold out, and deny your partner what they need, you end up without the possibility of him or her ever meeting you needs. If you try to win – and in winning make your partner lose – you may end up with no relationship at all.

This doesn't mean not having what you want. It doesn't mean being walked all over. It doesn't mean only one of you giving and the other never learning to give. What it does mean is that in the end, both of you need to reach the point where your joint happiness, rather than your individual gain, is the most important thing of all. Each of you has to believe that the needs of both of you are more important than anything else.

In particular, you must both have your Fundamental Needs equally met. It simply doesn't work if one of you feels valued at the expense of the other's self esteem. Or if one of you has control and, as a result, the other never makes any decisions. Or if one of you succeeds, the other considering themselves a failure. If these things happen, then in the end, perhaps after years or perhaps after decades, your relationship will either collapse or will fossilise where it stands. You will realise that you aren't going to get your needs met in this relationship, and that ultimately, your choice is to stay and have no influence over your life, or go and start a new relationship.

Making 'both of you' more important than 'each of you' isn't easy. It certainly isn't possible if you try to achieve it in one leap from a standing start of a history of painful arguments. It isn't possible if you have lost all trust in your relationship. It is possible, but more time-consuming, if only one of you is doing it, meanwhile waiting for the other to follow suit; as will happen if you're working through this book alone. And that's why this step has been left nearly to the end of the ten-step process.

You need to be clear about what you personally need. You need to react sympathetically, seriously and positively when your partner tells you his or her needs. You need to be willing to keep going and keep negotiating, until both of you, not just one of you, have what you want. You need to refuse, point blank, ever to settle for a solution that leaves either of you unhappy. And then you need to carry through that solution, without reneging, so that both of you are satisfied.

! ——————————— *Task 8.2* ————————————

Meet the need

Just once in the next week, spot something your partner needs and do it for him or her. Don't pull back, don't ask why, don't ask for thanks, just do it. Do it because you want your partner to be happy, and because you want your relationship to work.

(Forward to Step 10, page 183)

!

——————————— MAKING IT EASY ———————————

Once you know what you want, you need to motivate your partner to do it. The secret is quite simple: presenting what you want so that your partner can find it easy. Often, because what we want is vital to us, we describe it desperately, defensively, in a way that sounds difficult. Because we don't feel we deserve it, we hold back from making it sound wonderful, compelling or convincing. It's not surprising that sometimes partners are unconvinced.

Often, because we don't feel we deserve what we want, we hold back from making it sound compelling or convincing. Or, because what we want is vital to us, we describe it desperately, in a way that sounds difficult. This can be especially true around sex, when we can want to make love so much that we end up pressuring each other in a way that's a total turn-off; and then wonder why the passion's died.

Karl and Tracy have been going out for four weeks. Tracy works a lot of weekends. Karl wants to see her this Saturday.

What happens	What's happening underneath
Karl: 'When are we going to see each other again? It'd be nice if you didn't have to work all next weekend.'	He says what he doesn't want rather than what he wants – and also criticises her.
Tracy: 'Yeah, it would be great for me too. So?'	She feels criticised, but is still interested.
Karl: 'Well, it'd be good to spend some time together. Any time would do.'	He presents his need vaguely, even though he does have a particular plan in mind. and doesn't explain why it's important to him.
Tracy: 'I work late this Saturday, and do earlies on Sunday. What about Sunday afternoon?'	She's unsure what he wants, so simply gives him information.
Karl: 'Well, Sunday afternoon's not good for me, but I suppose it would do. Should we go bowling then, seeing as it'll have to be during the day?'	He's now objecting because her offer doesn't fit with his needs, even though he didn't tell her what his needs were.
Tracy: 'Give me a break, Karl. You know I don't like bowling.'	Karl's suggested something that he knows won't necessarily appeal to her, simply because he enjoys it. Tracy feels irritated.
Karl: ' It's a real shame you can't make Saturday. Can't you call in sick on Sunday? Or aren't I that important to you?'	He suggests something that she may well feel is wrong or inadvisable, then uses emotional blackmail to pressure her.
Tracy: 'I can't do that.'	She isn't willing to let down her work mates, and is quite angry he suggested it.
Karl: 'Well, OK, maybe I'll give you a ring later in the week and we can sort something out.'	He doesn't give any ground, and doesn't meet her halfway.
Tracy: 'OK.'	What's going through her head is 'I don't think so.'

In an attempt to get Tracy to do what he wants, Karl actually makes all the wrong moves.

He could have played it very differently.

What happens	What's happening underneath
Karl: 'When are we going to see each other again?'	He wants to know.
Tracy: 'When do you suggest?'	She's keen.
Karl: 'Well, I'd like us to go out at the weekend. Sunday isn't good for me. On Saturday, there's a band playing that I think you'd really get into. It'd be great to go out on a Saturday: it would make us feel like a real couple.'	He says what he wants specifically, positively, and enthusiastically. He also suggests something he thinks she would like. Finally, he expresses a real, underlying need: to be seen as a couple.
Tracy: 'Great, but there could be a problem. I work late on Saturday, and do earlies on Sunday.'	She's interested, but realises that it might not be possible.
Karl: 'Well, it sounds like you want to go, but it's just work that's the problem. I'm wondering if there's a way round this one. '	He moves towards a solution.
Tracy: 'I don't finish 'til eight on Saturday. I could make it, but only just.'	She feels he understands her problem, and wants to make it all work out.
Karl: 'If you really feel you can't, there's always another night. But if all you're worried about is the timing, why don't I pick you up from work and drive you home, to save time. Then if I took you to work on Sunday morning, you could get up later.'	He makes it clear that her concerns are important, takes them seriously, goes more than halfway to meet them.
Tracy: 'That's brilliant . . .'	She's getting the impression that she's important to him, and that if there's a problem in the relationship, they can work it out.

In the first conversation, Karl doesn't get the result he wants because he isn't clear about his needs. When he does eventually tell Tracy what he wants, he pressures her to meet those needs, ignores hers, and makes no attempt to get a working arrangement.

In the second conversation, Karl gets it right. He says clearly what his needs are, but he doesn't expect Tracy to meet them, or pressure her when she doesn't. He consistently makes her feel that she has a choice, and that he'll respect her choice. And, he tries hard to get an arrangement that works for both of them.

To motivate your partner, make sure that:

- Rather than presenting what you want vaguely, put some detail to your need, particularly explaining why you want it.
- Rather than offering or asking for something that you know won't appeal, where possible, ask for what you need from options that you know will please your partner.
- Rather than brushing aside what your partner needs, respect it and show you're working towards it.
- Rather than bringing up old complaints – particularly if there's been bad feeling from the start about this issue – concentrate on creating a solution
- Rather than pressuring, acting aggressively, or using emotional blackmail which will almost always mean your partner digs in their heels, acknowledge any worries or objections your partner has.
- Rather than making things difficult, actively offer support to make things as easy as possible for your partner to do what you want.

! ═══════════════ *Task 8.3* ═══════════════

Motivate me!

What would really motivate your partner to meet your needs? What would really motivate you to meet your partner's needs?

Think about this and if you can, swap notes with your partner. Give lessons in how you can best motivate each other.

(Forward to Step 10, page 184)   !

NEGOTIATING THE PEACE AGREEMENT

Solutions can be easy when, at bottom, your needs are the same. Karl and Tracy both wanted to see each other: it was just that the practicalities were so difficult that when Karl asked in an unhelpful way, Tracy dug her heels in. When he asked in a positive way, they soon found a solution. Sometimes, though, what each of you wants just doesn't quite match. You want to go to Spain, she wants to go to Egypt. He wants you to be tidier, you want to have the freedom to make a mess. You need to tackle things a slightly different way.

You need to negotiate. Real negotiation – working together so that both of you are happy – is the basis on which all truly successful relationships are created. It's also, interestingly, the basis on which all truly successful political settlements are made: high-ranking politicians nowadays have thorough training in negotiation skills. It involves communicating your real needs, expanding your options, looking closely at what works, finding a solution that suits you both, and then putting that into practice.

Be aware that if you're working through the book on your own, it may take a while to introduce these more formal negotiation methods into your relationship. The other recommendations made in this step will make a difference, however. Once they do, then gently suggest the strategies below one at a time, so that your partner can adopt them gradually.

Communicate your needs

When you decided what you wanted, you also considered your 'real needs': generalised things such as love, respect, value, control and success. One way out of any clash of wishes may be to consider the real needs that lie behind the specific things you think you want. If you can let go of specifics, and concentrate instead on meeting the more general 'real needs' you may find that your desires can be satisfied by something other than the particular elements that you're disagreeing about. That means you can often find a mutually acceptable solution much more easily.

For example, if the real need behind going to Spain is to speak a foreign language and the real need behind going to Egypt is to explore a very different culture, then perhaps a place that combines the two will suit. Ever been to Mexico?

Explore the evidence

If thinking more generally doesn't work, try thinking more specifically. When you decided what you wanted, you made sure that you defined what your needs were, what was important and what not. Use that information to explore just what each of you wants from your expressed option. Take each need and break it into its component parts. Be particular in specifying just what it is about each that appeals and what is irrelevant: the 'Must Haves' and the 'Don't Need to Haves'. Then, look at how you can combine them, to get an ideal that meets both sets of desires.

Perhaps you want to go to Spain because you need a rest. It doesn't matter where that break is, and the sun, sea and sand aren't vital. So pick and mix. Go on the Egyptian holiday, and add on the 'rest' element of the Spanish holiday: a week at home first, just sleeping.

Find more possibilities

When the two of you seem to have opposing needs, approaches, or solutions, you need to think up more possibilities. For so long as you're only dealing with two very different options, then each of you will choose one and stick to it. It's known in the negotiation trade as 'positioning'. If you can't resolve the issue, that just means you haven't thought of enough positions or possibilities. So create more. One of the new possibilities might appeal to both of you. Even if doesn't, it might by the time you've forty possible options rather than two and you'll feel far more optimistic that there can be a solution that will suit you both.

If the issue is Spain or Egypt, think up as many other holiday destinations as you can. Consider what possibilities are missing from the ones you've thought of. Take a large piece of paper and fill it with ideas. Find a large map and a pin. Brainstorm at least forty holiday destinations; all accepted, no rejections, even the silly ones. Ring a few friends and ask them to make suggestions.

Add in resources

It could be that what you need are more resources: more time or money, advice or support. This is particularly likely where arguments are linked to sexual problems which, in our culture at least, are rarely admitted, let alone discussed, and for which you may need the help of an expert therapist.

So if the choice is between Spain and Eygpt, it could be that the only problem is that you haven't got the money to do both this year. Is it possible to work overtime to get the money? Is it possible to stay with friends? Could a friendly local travel agent show you a cheap way round your problem?

Sort the pros and cons

Sometimes what you want has pros and cons. Particularly if you're trying to make a decision that has long-term implications – such as where to live, what jobs to take – then 'unpacking' the options can leave you both agreed on a solution. So go into more detail about the alternatives. Find out more information. List out the pros and cons on paper. So long as you keep emotions calm rather than stormy, and avoid saying things like 'My way has more pros and less cons than your way does', then you may both come to a common conclusion.

Once the holiday brochures are in, you could find that Egypt is too expensive for either of you. Affordable Spain suddenly becomes the option you both prefer.

Balance out wants

You're both committed to meeting both sets of needs equally. But do these needs have to be met together? Why not let one of you go to Spain, while the other goes to Egypt? Then meet your mutual need for time together by spending Christmas alone in a secluded cottage.

A variation on this is 'splitting down the middle': you both have what you want but not necessarily at once. Go on a cheap package tour to Spain this year, so you can save money and go to Egypt next year.

Experiment

Why not choose one option, then just try it and see? This is a particularly useful strategy if the issue is one where there aren't two alternatives, but a single possibility that one of you wants and the other doesn't.

So one of you wants to live in Spain, rather than just holiday there? Experiment by going for a working holiday. Then, with the information you've gathered, talk again about your thoughts, feelings and needs. If necessary, extend the experiment until you're both agreed on what you want.

Set up safety nets

What if experimenting isn't possible? Don't burn your bridges in the process of keeping one person happy. Often the other is hesitating, not because they don't want to go for a particular option, but because they are sensibly cautious. Their wariness alone, rather than any contradictory needs, leads them to disagree. If so, set up safety nets.

What if the once-in-a-lifetime offer of a Spanish villa is on the table, and has to be taken up now? Would the hesitater be happy to live in Spain for a year's trial, with an agreement to sell if they're not happy then? Could you make back-up plans, financial and emotional, for if the hesitater's worst fears are realised? If you can, then the issue may be easily resolved.

!═══════════════ *Task 8.4* ═══════════════

Playing negotiation

NB: This is a task to do only if you can swap notes with your partner

Take one tiny issue in your lives at the moment where you want slightly different things. Don't attempt to fully negotiate about it. Instead, just imagine you are negotiating.

Run through the strategies for negotiation – communicating, exploring, finding possibilities, adding resources, sorting the pros and cons, balancing wants, experimenting, setting up safety nets.

Whatever you decide isn't a real decision; don't put it into practice unless you feel it works.

(Forward to Step 10, page 184)

!

MAKING IT WORK

'When we met, I was still out in the country where I'd lived until my first husband died. He was in London; his kids had only just left home. When we decided to move in together, there were things about each other's places that we hated. He thought my place was too small, I thought his place was too new. He needed to be able to travel into London. I didn't want to move into the city. In the end, he moved up to where I live, but near the main-line station. Then we sold both our places and looked for somewhere we both wanted. It took ages, and we almost lost heart, but we stuck at it, changed the deal a few dozen times. And got what we wanted.' Liz

You've reached a solution to your issue. What you must do now is put it into practice and make it work. The bottom line is this: if you want your partner to rediscover hope in you, agree a solution that suits you both. If you want your partner to rediscover trust in you, then do what you've agreed: cheerfully, lovingly and on time.

Check that you're both truly happy

Sometimes you agree things, but the agreement's not quite genuine. Particularly if one of you specialises in appeasement, and likes to feel everyone is happy, then she may agree to a solution before she's actually gained what she wants. Then, mysteriously, problems and resentments will appear.

So it's wise to check. As you move from agreement to action, check that both of you are satisfied. Do either of you still feel uncomfortable: maybe tense, or with a churning stomach? Is your partner still a little withdrawn, unable to meet your eyes? Are either of you saying things like: 'If you want to . . . Well, if that's the only way . . . Well, nothing can be worse than fighting.'

It can be tempting, particularly after a long and tiring negotiation, to just plough on and ignore these signals. Don't. In the long term, it will backfire.

Instead, go back and find out what both of you want. Then reuse all the solutions suggested in this step to make sure that both of you're getting just that. Don't move forward until eye contact, smiles and general good feeling tell you that the agreement is one you're both completely satisfied with.

Log your agreement

Whether you're a new couple and just learning to solve problems together, or an experienced couple whose conflicts have rocked your trust, it's often wise to write down what you've decided. That way you both know what has to happen.

Together, make a note of what you've decided. Include what each of you has agreed to do, what times this has to be done by, and other important details such as location, schedule or budget. Keep this agreement in a safe place. If it involves things that you need to remember to do, particularly on a regular basis, you may also want to add reminders, strategically placed. A sticky note on the toaster may remind you to clear the crumbs because your partner worries about the fire risk. An 'alarm call' on the computer may remind you to phone home because your partner likes to talk to you at lunchtime.

❗ ============== *Task 8.5* ==============

Practising negotiation

NB: This is a task to do only if you can swap notes with your partner.

Next time you, as a couple, are discussing something where you have different needs, use all the guidelines in this step to reach a solution.

Find out what your individual needs are. Motivate each other. Negotiate and put that negotiation into practice.

Over the next month, negotiate at least three times.

(Forward to Step 10, page 184)

❗

Monitor

Your solution, however well negotiated, may not be a solution that works. So it's wise to set a date – or a series of dates – when you look back at your agreement and find out what's happening.

Perhaps both of you have done what you agreed, but one or both of you isn't happy. However content the other partner is, this means that something has to change.

Perhaps one or both of you haven't done what you agreed. This is tricky. Occasionally it means that the defaulting partner had no intention of carrying through the plan, and is just being manipulative. If so, you do need to face squarely the possibility that there is a serious lack of commitment and goodwill in your relationship.

But usually, what defaulting means is that you feel what is happening is wrong for you, unfair or just impossible. Usually, you've felt like that at the beginning. It would have been better in the long run, if less comfortable short term, to have said so from the start. Or, perhaps since the original negotiation, one of you has changed his or her mind. You were happy, but now you're not. What's happening has given you more information or convinced you that this plan isn't viable.

In all these cases, what's needed is re-negotiation. You both need to pay particular attention to whether you're happy with what's agreed. Don't panic. If you stick with it, then almost certainly you'll find something that works.

WHERE ARE YOU NOW?

Step 8 has helped you gain skills in negotiating so that both of you have what you want from your relationship.

As you complete the tasks in this step, remember to turn to Step 10 on pages 183–184 and fill in the relevant sections there.

Move on to Step 9 when:

- you believe that the happiness of both of you is more important than your own individual happiness.

- you've resolved issues successfully several times. (If you're working through the book alone, allow yourself extra time to allow what you're doing to encourage your partner to start to learn how to resolve issues too.)

- you've begun to feel sure that the ways you're using to resolve your issues mean that the relationship is going to give you both more of what you want.

TROUBLE-PROOF THE FUTURE

'We'd been a year without real trouble when we had the shock of our lives. Andrew's son Dean came back from America and stayed for two weeks; and we were right back into the arguments again. I think in hindsight that we'd forgotten just how he used to stir things up so much. Certainly I'd forgotten just how threatened I felt because Andrew and his son are so close. But Dean had only been in the house a matter of hours when we were up in our bedroom hissing at each other just like the old days. Then we just looked at one another aghast and said "What are we doing?". It was good for us in a way. We'll never sit back on our laurels again.' Jenny

When relationships improve, there's often the sense that nothing will ever go wrong again. Maybe you've weathered your first week without a quarrel. Maybe you've had a month of sheer happiness. You feel good: not just

---

! ═══════════════ *Task 9.1* ═══════════════

Future prospects

Imagine a year has passed, and you've solved your conflict problems. You've put into practice everything you've learned in this book, and made it work for you.

    What will life be like? Be realistic, but optimistic.

    What will you be doing . . . thinking . . . feeling? How will life be different: at work . . . at play . . . at home . . . in bed . . . on holiday? What will be the best thing about life? What will be the best thing about your love life?

    Now, think about what you can do to make it happen.

(Forward to Step 10, page 184) **!**

about conflict management, but about yourself, about your partner, about the relationship, about life.

However wonderful the improvement, though, it isn't the entire answer. For almost certainly, at some time in the future, there'll be further problems. Maybe, slowly, you'll feel yourself sliding into irritation. Maybe, suddenly and without warning, there'll be a furious fight. Maybe there'll be no obvious conflict; but instead, disagreements will somehow never be aired, issues mysteriously never be resolved.

This is normal. Reversals do happen, even when you've made a genuine improvement in your relationship. The issue isn't whether you ever have reversals, but whether you can recover from them. That is why you have to trouble-proof the future. You have to make sure that whatever happens, you can still get firmly back on track again.

There may be three reasons why you might begin moving into conflict again after you thought you'd stopped. First, there may be something seriously wrong with your relationship which all the conflict management techniques in the world can't resolve. Or, you've let panic take hold; a slight problem has turned into a major one because it's startled you into forgetting the skills you've learned and reverting to your old ways of behaving. Or, maybe you aren't mine-detecting argument triggers – so they catch you unawares.

ARE YOU IN REAL TROUBLE?

This book aims to help relationships where what causes conflict is lack of understanding or skill. Perhaps, like most people, you've never learned how to handle disagreement. Or perhaps you've never understood what's happening when you fight. No wonder things have gone wrong. But once you have the knowledge and the skill, there's no reason why things shouldn't go right.

This book doesn't presume to help where what causes conflict is on a much deeper level. Perhaps the two of you have completely different life directions: you want kids and she doesn't, and actually, having kids is far more important than having each other. Or you have completely different needs: you want stability and he wants freedom and actually those needs are so deep-rooted that you don't know how to start negotiations.

The following signals indicate that this may be true for you:

- You argue almost every time you're in each other's company, aggressively and with no way of resolving the issues.
- More often than not, your arguments lead to verbal and physical violence.
- Your relationship is lived out against a background of alcoholism, drug addiction, compulsive gambling or other extremely painful behaviours.
- One or both of you is having an affair, so not actually putting most of your energy into your main relationship.
- One or both of you hates the other most of the time, not just in the middle of an argument.
- One or both of you thinks or talks about leaving most of the time, not just in the middle of an argument.
- One or both of you has actually decided to leave, and is following the suggestions made in this book simply to keep up appearances.

If even some of these things are true, or become true in the future, then find further support. You may want to talk through your problems with people who know you. You may, as suggested earlier, want to turn to counsellors who can give you unbiased and ongoing help to sort out what you want. At any rate, take some time, alone or with your partner, to think and talk through what you need to do next.

But don't panic. All this doesn't mean the two of you have to split up – or that you're going to. Many a couple seemingly on the rocks are, ten years after a relationship crisis, together and much happier than they were before. What it does mean is that you must find further help if you're to have the relationship you want and deserve.

__WHEN YOU PUSH THE PANIC BUTTON__

'Things are so much better now than they used to be. But I do tend to feel desperate even if we simply get a bit irritable with each other. I tend to think that because we spent so long fighting, if we slip just

*once, we'll be back to square one again. And often, it's my
desperation that stirs things up and makes us even more likely to
argue. I have to remember that we've beaten it once. We can do it
again.'* Leigh

When you're just learning how to manage conflict, it may be
a struggle. But there is often a constant sense of hope and
achievement as you meet with increasing success.

But when you've gained that success and believe you've left
the problems behind you, if something goes wrong you may
panic. If you have an argument or a spate of arguments, you may
begin to think that this is the start of a renewed deterioration. If
you do think this, and if you do become tense about your
relationship, then this in itself will make it more likely that things
will get worse.

The hard fact is that you will have another argument again at
some time in your life. It will probably be sooner rather than later.
And what you do is this. Quite simply, stop as soon as you realise
what is happening. If this is in the middle of the fight, use any of
the techniques you've learned to drive the argument back towards
good feeling. If you lose control of the process, then take time out.
But as soon as you can, with or without your partner, work to
regain your confidence. One slip doesn't mean to say that you've
failed.

Six things to remember if you start arguing again:

- 'This is normal. There's never been a relationship between two
  people that didn't have some conflict.'
- 'Last time we avoided an argument, we did something that
  worked. There's no reason why we can't do that again.'
- 'If we can cope this time, then we'll know for certain that we
  can cope if it happens again.'
- 'This fight will help us remember that we need to spot triggers
  ahead of time – and so make it less likely we'll fight again.'
- 'Just because we've argued, that doesn't mean to say that we're
  bad people, or have a bad relationship.'
- 'To really master conflict management, we at least need to
  have one or two conflicts.'

This final point is an important one. You can learn so much when
you hit conflict. You increase your knowledge and understanding.

You have the opportunity to practise all the skills you've learned. And you can take things further. You can develop techniques that are personal to you, strategies that work because you alone have created them.

What if you need extra help to survive a difficult patch? Relate offers not only long-term counselling but also a counselling help line, and one-off trouble-shooting sessions. Details are in the Appendix. Through these, you can quickly find support for the backlash you may feel after a particularly bad quarrel.

! ================= *Task 9.2* =================

Reserve parachute

NB: This is a task to do only if you can swap notes with your partner.

Flip back through the book. Choose one conflict management technique – the simplest and fastest-acting you can – that has already worked well for you.

Write this technique down on a piece of paper, and underneath write: 'This worked for us once. It can work for us again.' Put that paper somewhere safe.

If things become difficult, you may not remember what to do; panic can cause your brain to go on strike. If so, reach for that piece of paper. Read it. Use the technique.

(Forward to Step 10, page 184) **!**

THE IMPORTANCE OF
_____MINE-DETECTING_____

'It was one of those weeks from hell. Lynne had just had to do a big rush job at work, I'd had a short week at the factory, and she'd started taking the pill again. When we found ourselves screaming about who'd folded the newspaper the wrong way, it hit us that maybe we'd let things go a bit far. We started having more sleep. That helped a lot.'
Mick

Doing well can be dangerous: you may leave yourself open to conflict triggers simply because you don't think you need to guard against them. You may not even notice that the vulnerability factors are building up. You need to mine-detect regularly.

!=============== *Task 9.3* ===============

Make a date

NB: This is a task to do only if you can swap notes with your partner.

Decide together, as a couple, how often you feel you need to 'touch down' about your relationship. Arrange a regular day, time and place. Make a date with each other that will continually build your relationship.

(Forward to Step 10, page 184)

!

One useful suggestion is to sit down together regularly to do a brief 'where are we at?' check on the relationship. Once a week is ideal. Studies have shown that married couples who have such weekly meetings are far less likely to divorce. The two of you can review any triggers that might be looming, look ahead to future events that might be stressful, and review your thoughts and feelings. Of course this doesn't mean to say you shouldn't deal with issues as they come up. And where a life change looms, you may want to have longer meetings to keep pace with all the shifts that are happening.

You could use this check-list as the basis for your regular touching base.

- How are we doing? Feeling disillusioned . . . angry . . . frightened . . . accepting and loving?
- Are we tired . . . stressed . . . under pressure?
- Are we having enough quality time together . . . enough time and space alone?
- Have there been any shifts in health . . . hormone levels . . . alcohol consumption?
- Has there been a recent traumatic event or dramatic change in our lives: accident . . . illness . . . bereavement?
- Is anyone from outside the relationship (including the children) influencing us, and making us more likely to argue?

- Is there a stressful period approaching: a big project at work, a celebration, exam, house move?
- Are we coming up to a life change of any kind: wedding, birth, career shift, children leaving, retirement?
- Are there any emotions that either of us wants to express? (Remember to use 'I feel').
- Are there any current issues that either of us wants to resolve?
- Is it time to check progress on any issues that we've recently negotiated?
- Are there any far-future issues that either of us want to start discussing now: planning to work abroad, job shift, starting a family?

For each point, check out what's happening. If there's a problem, ask what you can do about that. Where you can, take practical action. Get support where you need it. Sort things out as quickly as possible.

! ═══════════════ *Task 9.4* ═══════════════

Enjoying your relationship

A final safeguard to trouble-shooting the future is this. As you spend less time arguing, spend more quality time with your partner. As you diminish the bad feeling, build the good feeling. Start a deliberate policy of enjoyment. Talk, snuggle or make love. Play to offset all the hard work you've been doing on your relationship. Celebrate: because after all you've been through, you deserve to.

This very week, do something enjoyable with your partner. If you're working through the book alone, you don't have to tell him or her that this is a task you've been set. It doesn't have to be anything expensive: an evening with a good video, a walk in the park, a special meal. But it should allow you to be together, alone, relaxing, enjoying yourselves and each other.

!

You can also use this meeting to make sure that you're maintaining progress on your skills. As you change, your reasons for coming into conflict will change, and so will your ways of managing your conflicts, so use Steps 2 and 3 to track your progress. Also, keep in touch with your feelings: use Steps 4, 5, and 6 to use emotions as a barometer to when things are going well and badly, and as an energy source for taking action. Finally, keep communicating and negotiating: use Steps 7 and 8 to talk through issues and then resolve them.

The key to trouble-proofing the future is to see conflict management as a long-term project. You don't have to be perfect immediately. You can build up your mastery slowly. You can gradually increase your understanding. You can practise the skills over time. You can, in short, continuously develop a win-win style of sorting out your problems.

WHERE ARE YOU NOW?

Step 9 has helped you weather any future problems you might hit as you start to consolidate your conflict management.

As you complete the tasks in this step, remember to turn to Step 10 and fill in the relevant sections there.

You'll have completed the ten-step process when:

- you've thought through the possibility that something more serious than conflict management techniques may be needed in your relationship – and taken any relevant action.

- you've spent a conflict-free period where you've been able to avoid or reduce bad feeling and to settle your differences and disagreements by communication and negotiation.

- you've faced and survived at least one more argument without panicking, and learned from that experience.

- you've started to build into your relationship some ways in which you enjoy each other's company.

When you feel you've done all this, read the Afterword at the end of Step 10.

ACT ON WHAT YOU HAVE DISCOVERED AND LEARNED

You can't change yourself or your relationship just by thinking. You have to act. Step 10 brings together all the other steps, making a record of your actions, and reminding yourself of what you've promised to do.

It will help to review this action record regularly: not only as you work through the steps, but also after you've finished them and are practising to improve your conflict management. It's a constant record of all you've achieved, and how far you've come.

Make a note of your answers to the following questions.

STEP 1

Three things I want to change about our ways of resolving conflict are (from 1.1):

Three things I will be doing differently once we've changed are:

My goal is to have made these improvements by this date (from 1.2):

STEP 2

Three things I have now understood about why we argue are:

One lifestyle factor that's currently affecting our argument rate is:

This is what I am doing to solve it (from 2.1):

One person who is badly affecting the way I handle conflict for the worse is:

This is what I'm doing to reduce the bad effect this person is having (from 2.2):

One 'payoff' that I might be gaining from arguments is:

This is what I'm doing to have my needs met in other ways: (from 2.3):

One problematic way in which I and my partner think differently about 'how relationships have to be' is:

This is what I am doing to be more tolerant of this difference (from 2.4):

One life change that I or we have been through and which may be adding to our conflict is:

This is what I am doing to cope better with this life change (from 2.5):

One deeper concern or Fundamental Need I have that's leading to arguments at the moment is:

This is one thing I am doing to make a start in solving these issues (from 2.6):

STEP 3

Three things I now understand about the way we as a couple argue are:

One way of handling conflict that I borrowed from a person in my past and am trying not to use any more is (from 3.1):

My personal conflict pattern is a mixture of these styles:

This is one thing I'm going to change about that (from 3.2):

Our couple conflict pattern contains these styles:

This is one thing I'm going to change about that (from 3.3):

STEP 4

Three things I now understand about the way I use my emotions are:

Of the three unhelpful ways to handle emotion, I tend to most use:

The unhelpful ways I handle emotion vary according to (from 4.1):

These are some notes on what I have learned by trying to handle my emotions helpfully:

These are three successes I have had when trying to handle my emotions helpfully (from 4.2):

Some emotional time bombs that may be lurking in our relationship are:

This is what I am doing to defuse these time bombs (from 4.3): (NB: This is a task to do only if you feel that there are emotional time bombs in your relationship.)

STEP 5

Three things I now re-understand about my partner are:

One way in which my partner is different from me that I now realise has made the relationship better is (from 5.1):

One fear that I now recognise in my partner is (from 5.2):

One of my partner's panic buttons that I will try not to push in future is: (from 5.3):

One way I can try out to reduce my partner's fear is:

This is one thing I learned when I tried it (from 5.3):

One issue which we have now forgiven each other for is (from 5.4): (NB: This is a task to do only if you feel that there are forgiveness issues in your relationship.)

STEP 6

Three things I now understand about ways to drive our arguments are:

Three ways I know ahead of time that an argument is going to happen are (from 6.1):

Number one on my 'on my own' list of good strategies is:

This is one thing I learned when I tried it (from 6.2):

The strategy we're going to try out together is:

This is how we are going to remind each other to use the strategy:

This is one thing we learned when we tried it (from 6.3):
(NB: This is a task to do only if you can swap notes with your partner.)

_____STEP 7_____

Three things I now understand about communicating with my partner are:

One thing I've learned from sitting down with my partner and taking turns to communicate is (from 7.1):
(NB: This is a task to do only if you can swap notes with your partner.)

One thing I learned about listening to my partner in the course of normal conversation is (from 7.2):

One thing I learned about talking to my partner in the course of normal conversation is (from 7.3):

_____STEP 8_____

Three things I now understand about resolving the issue are:

The thing I gave myself as a treat this week is:

It felt good because (from 8.1):

The thing I did for my partner this week is:

This is how I felt after I'd done it (from 8.2):

One way I can try to motivate my partner to meet my needs is:

This is one thing I learned when I tried it (from 8.3):

One thing I learned when we practised negotiating together is (from 8.4):
(NB: This is a task to do only if you can swap notes with your partner.)

One thing I learned when we negotiated together on a real issue is (from 8.5):
(NB: This is a task to do only if you can swap notes with your partner.)

STEP 9

Three things I now understand about trouble-proofing the future are:

One thing I have decided to do to create good future prospects is (from 9.1):

This is the conflict management technique we chose to write down and keep as a reserve parachute for when we have another argument (from 9.2):
(NB: This is a task to do only if you can swap notes with your partner.)

Our arrangement about regular touchdowns to build our relationship is – day, time and place (from 9.3):
(NB: This is a task to do only if you can swap notes with your partner.)

One thing we have done this week to enjoy our relationship is (from 9.4):

AFTERWORD

If all goes well, this book will be the start of a pain-free relationship for you.

As you know, it won't be the start of a partnership with no differences, no disagreements – or no conflict. But while conflict will still be there, you'll handle it better than before. You'll understand why it's happening, and why it's happening as it is. You'll spot destructive conflict before it happens, and head it off at the pass. You'll no longer need to handle it by lashing out, or backing down. You'll be able to listen to your partner's feelings, and appreciate them. You'll give and receive easily, and negotiate whenever needs aren't being met. In short, you'll be using a win-win conflict style as opposed to all the other, less effective options. You'll stop arguing and start talking – and as a result, you'll become more and more loving.

There is one more thing you can do. You can pass on what you have learned.

For as you know, you're not alone in having had difficulty coping with conflict. You're not alone in never having been taught to handle it. Very few people are ever shown how to resolve relationship disagreements – and that is one reason why so many people have unhappy relationships.

But you can break the chain. You can show and tell those around you – your children perhaps, or your friends and family – that it is possible to disagree and not fight, to have differences and not lash out. You can show them that differences and disagreements are not threatening so long as they can be resolved.

For the best lesson you can take from this book is that conflict can be managed constructively.

And the best gift you can pass on from this book is to show other people, through the way you love, that the lesson the book offers is a lesson worth learning.

FURTHER READING

You may want to take the ideas explored in this book further. If so, these books may interest you:

The RELATE Guide to Better Relationships (about building relationships) by Sarah Litvinoff. Vermilion, ISBN: 0-09-177432-2

The RELATE Guide to Staying Together (reclaiming love after relationship crisis) by Susan Quilliam. Vermilion, ISBN: 0-09-179007-7

The RELATE Guide to Sex in Loving Relationships (improving your sex life) by Sarah Litvinoff. Vermilion, ISBN: 0-09-175294-9

The RELATE Guide to Second Families (dealing with stepfamilies) by Suzie Hayman. Vermilion, ISBN: 0-09-181358-1

If your explorations in Step 1 have led you to consider breaking up, then you may want to read:

The RELATE Guide to Starting Again (surviving marriage breakup) by Sarah Litvinoff. Vermilion, ISBN: 0-09-175295-7

All of the above can be ordered from TBS Direct on 01206 255800

Particularly if, after reading Step 2, you recognise that you need extra help in some area of your life as an individual or a couple, these books may be helpful:

Managing Stress by Ursula Markham. Element Books, ISBN: 1-85230-631-9

Working Mother, A Practical Handbook for the Nineties by Sarah Litvinoff and Marianne Velmans. Pocket Books, ISBN: 0-671-71540-2

Hormone Dilemma: should you take HRT? by Susan Love and Karen Lindsay. Thorsons, ISBN: 0-7225-3429-9

When Parents Die by Rebecca Abrams. Thorsons, ISBN: 0-7225-3131-1

Comfort in Bereavement by William Purcell. Canterbury Press, ISBN: 1-85311-148-1

Crunch Points for Couples (help in coping with life change) by Julia Cole. Sheldon Press, ISBN: 0-85969-743-6

Particularly if, after reading Steps 4 or 5, you realise that you or your partner have needs that can't be met by this book alone, you may find these books of use:

The Courage to Heal (coming to terms with sexual abuse) by Ellen Bass and Laura Davis. Cedar, ISBN: 0-7493-0938-5

Off the Hook (alcoholism and other addictions) by Corinne Sweet. Piatkus Books, ISBN: 0-7499-1311-8

Dealing with Depression by The Samaritans with Trevor Barnes. Vermilion, ISBN: 0-09-181363-8

relate

building better relationships

Relate is a national registered charity with 60 years' experience in helping people with their relationships.

Relate offers counselling and sex therapy to help with difficulties in marriage or in any adult couple relationship. People can turn to Relate for help whether or not they are married and whatever their age, race, personal beliefs, sexual orientation or social background.

Counselling is available for couples or individuals. We can help if you are having problems and want to work them out, or if you want to separate, or if your relationship has ended.

Sex therapy is available for couples or individuals who have specific sexual problems.

Counselling and sex therapy are private and confidential forms of help.

Relate's counsellors are carefully selected and trained by Relate to a nationally recognised standard. They receive continuing support and supervision and have access to a range of professional consultants. In this way Relate maintains consistently high standards.

There are 126 Relate Centres in England, Wales and Northern Ireland. Each Relate Centre is an independent organisation which is registered as a charity in its own name. All the Centres are affiliated to National Relate and abide by its standards.

To find your local Centre, look up Relate in the telephone directory.

A list of other Relate titles also published by Vermilion can be found on page 186.

INDEX